The **Revitalization** of the AMERICAN CLASSROOM

Thomas R. Shipley EdD

© *Thomas R. Shipley, EdD*
thomshipleybooks@hotmail.com
www.thomshipleybooks.com

Copyright © 2014 **Authored By** Thomas R. Shipley EdD

ISBN: 1494390264
ISBN 13: 9781494390266
Library of Congress Control Number: 2013923499
CreateSpace Independent Publishing Platform
North Charleston, South Carolina

*An inexpensive, briefly stated, common-sense approach
that will breathe new life and vitality into the traditional
American classroom*

Thomas R. Shipley has served as an elementary school teacher, a high school teacher, a high school administrator, the first coordinator of educational information systems for a county district, and the first chief information officer for the Maryland State Department of Education, one of the most respected state departments of education in the nation. He retired from there as the acting assistant superintendent of schools, and has spent decades as an advisor and consultant to the House and Senate Committees on Education. He has served as the executive director of a billion-dollar-plus national education funding association, as well as serving on and chairing several national education committees.

THOMAS R. SHIPLEY, EdD
thomshipleybooks@hotmail.com
www.thomshipleybooks.com
2014

CONTENTS

Foreword

When I finally finished writing this book, I was pleased with the content and thought that I had finally documented something refreshing and meaningful; I had shed some new light on an otherwise rather dark and gloomy situation.

Not so! At least, not "new" light.

After editing one of the chapters, a dear friend sent me a cartoon with a quote that I had never heard before. It was both embarrassing and refreshing. Here, someone had already summarized my thoughts, observations, and analysis:

> *"…if you judge a fish by its ability to climb a tree, it will live its whole life believing that it is stupid."*
> *–Albert Einstein*

I was, at first, embarrassed because I had assumed that my ideas were, relevant, current, accurate—perhaps even original. I suddenly find that they were not nearly as new as I had once thought. I was especially embarrassed because I now knew that we as educators had been warned about this fallacy almost one hundred years ago, and yet we have done little to heed the warning. Teacher-training institutions have mostly perpetuated the idea of a lockstep curriculum, which violates the premise of Einstein's observation. These institutions have the responsibility for training professionals for what is probably the most important job in society.

Please don't recoil! I do mean "the most important." Just think a little deeper about the intended role of the teacher. Where would the world be—from a child in a grass hut in the Amazon to the halls of Oxford—without someone from the previous generation passing on accumulated information, techniques, and knowledge to the next?

On the other hand, I was refreshed and even enthused because I realized that this book is, in fact, about something critical, current, and achievable. I felt validated because I have synthesized decades of observations, experiences, and behaviors that have proven to be workable solutions toward my learning the art and technique of being a successful classroom teacher.

In this book, we will discuss teacher qualifications, teacher training, and teacher evaluations. We will examine the rationale and the technique for evaluating what's going on in the classroom and offer specific steps toward identifying and correcting weaknesses. We will focus on—indeed, insist on—the need for the teacher to be a highly respected subject-matter expert; an authority on the subject he or she is teaching. Lastly, we will explain why that is relevant to the whole revitalization effort.

When you finish *The Revitalization of the American Classroom*, you will see how necessary these changes are, how fundamental they are, how easy they are to implement, and what little monetary investment is needed. This book is a fun read, an easy read, and, I hope, a thought-provoking, revitalization journey.

Introduction

For the best part of eighty years, I have observed and analyzed—from almost every vantage point imaginable—the plight of our American public education system.

I have watched through the eyes of a skinny, introverted young boy, living through one wasted year after another, and I have watched as an excited, energetic, well-behaved, inquisitive teenager. Through it all, however, I was rarely comfortable as a student. I always felt that I was just going through the motions, unrecognized for what I had to offer, and never understood for how I learned. Being aggressive or debating established practices with a teacher wasn't (until college) in my nature. Even though I wanted to be in school and was motivated and inquisitive, I was rarely recognized for what experiences I could have brought to the classroom. In retrospect, few teachers recognized my potential. One teacher who did, however, changed my life, and she will forever be loved, remembered, and appreciated.

I have also watched through the eyes of a father of four alert youngsters, and later, through the same experiences of nine grandchildren, all reliving the same weak and misguided education, generation after generation.

Lastly, I have watched through the eyes of a dedicated, experienced, and very successful educator: an educator who slowly but surely refused to accept those traditional behaviors, methods, and practices that created the conspicuous inefficiencies to which our students are exposed every day. I watched as easily identifiable and easily fixable shortcomings were blindly recycled, keeping the public school education from being the great experience it should have been, that it must become. Call it enhancement, improvement, correction, or revitalization—you pick the adjective—the elimination of our shortcomings is necessary (indeed, is critical) for all children, for our suffering economy, and for the overall health of our nation.

Make no mistake about it! If global warming, pollution, famine, poverty, water shortages, and cancer are to be resolved before it's too late, it will be done by students who are this very day sitting in your classroom. The future of the nation, the culture, and indeed the civilization, is in the hands of our teachers.

For many decades, parents, board members, and school superintendents have repeatedly begged their governing bodies for more money. These well-meaning people genuinely believed that more money would produce better education. In almost every case, these requests are accompanied by written proposals and cost justifications that resulted in megabuck infusions year after year. These justifications quietly (sometimes mysteriously) fade away, and are eventually abandoned, with no long-lasting, positive result and rarely a report admitting their failure. Innovations are ushered in with the fanfare of a trumpet, and brushed away with a feather duster. Few if any express concern.

Classroom after classroom have relived the same problems under different umbrellas of jargon and hype. The costs continue to go up—the results continue (in many cases) to go down. When the educators and the public recognize the failure of these proposals, they all take a deep breath, roll their eyes, and allow the original cycle to continue. Somehow, we must break the cycle. Revitalization demands a systemic approach. No one person, no single isolated change, from the color of the walls to the salary of the teacher, will break the cycle. Education is an integrated and systemic endeavor. If you have a backyard pond in which your expensive koi are sick, you will not solve your problem by adding more lilies. No single-variable discussion is relevant. Our problems are much bigger than any stand-alone adjustment can correct.

Some years it was "higher salaries," and some years it was "back to the basics." Some years it was "we need more technology," and a few years later "we need more personal intervention and understanding." Accountability is frequently discussed as if it's a new responsibility. Bureaucrats demand it, and unions mistakenly fight the use of the very word. We have read about and discussed ad infinitum studies on "Why Johnny Can't Read" and "Why Johnny Can't Write," we debate the merits of homework and parental involvement, but we are embarrassed and reluctant to address the one real issue: "Why Teachers Can't Teach." Is it Johnny...or is it us? Will higher salaries make better teachers and more money assure higher test scores? There is a clear distinction between the art of *investing* money for education and the process of *spending* money in the name of education. There is an equally clear distinction between teachers being certified and being qualified, of being degreed to teach and being prepared to teach.

While acting as the state assistant superintendent for business and finance, I saw firsthand the difference between spending and investing. There's seldom a direct correlation between per-pupil costs and educational outcomes. Before seeking higher taxes and bigger budgets, we must first learn to do a better job with the money we do have.

Regardless of the curriculum, regardless of the subject being taught, most of our problems can be identified and solved with nothing more than a better understanding of how kids learn and how teachers teach. This must be the top agenda item for all educators who embrace teaching as their calling, as their career, as their profession. This must also be at the top of the agenda for the first faculty meeting of the coming year.

At this point, there is no reason for a discussion on the need for more money. We are already disproportionately outspending other industrialized, civilized societies—outspending them with less efficiency and poorer results. It's time to stop embarrassing ourselves. We must do something different; we must break the cycle.

—∞∞∞—

In the following pages, I invite you to explore with me the possibility that all of the major problems in the classrooms can be identified and remediated with reasonable, easy-to-learn, proven practices. They can be improved without new jargon or gadgets, without additional money, and, most important, with (in almost every case) the existing staff of enthusiastic, revitalized teachers and administrators.

We will explore and discuss the relationship between the failing state of education and the role of failing teacher-training institutions; the result of poorly trained professionals—in contrast to our having bad teachers. Please, *read that again,* because *this* is the core of the problem. Many poor teachers are not even aware of their inadequacies—of the poor training for which they paid so dearly. They are working diligently every day, but with dubious results. Most have been shortchanged by the very teaching institutions that are responsible for perpetuating America's educational weaknesses. Majoring in education should not be known around the campus as "an easy degree." Only the smartest and the wisest should even consider becoming educators.

Many principals are fine administrators, but are not equipped as educators. Without a doubt, a well-run school must have a great administrator. Each school is a business, requiring an effective CEO. As administrators, they do well to get thousands of youngsters to the desired subject, in the right room, with the right teacher, at the correct time. They may keep the school budget balanced, the building heated, and the PTA running smoothly. They may hire and occasionally fire teachers and support staff, attend district meetings, and negotiate discipline problems. Do they, however, have the time, the experience, the training, the understanding, or even the authority to be educators? Can they get beyond the required daily administrative task of running a school into evaluating what's going on in (sometimes hundreds of) classrooms, into each teacher's performance? Should they even have responsibilities and expectations beyond administration?

While it is errantly assumed otherwise, the superintendent of a complex construction site cannot monitor every nail or rivet that is set on the job. There is a point at which we must admit (somewhat contrary to today's legal leanings) that the worker being paid to deliver the rivet or wield the hammer has the primary responsibility to the chosen profession, for the quality of the job being delivered.

Most teachers cling to the traditional methods, mimicking with religious fervor the way they were taught. By that very dedication, most think that they are doing the children a great service. Unfortunately, the methods they cling to were equally unproductive when *they* were students. Nevertheless, cling they will. Traditions are comfortable, easy, and perceived by others from the same camp to be effective.

The suggestions in this book are intended for a wide audience. Education is not a topic that is relevant only to those "in the business." ***The success of our public education system affects the health of the entire nation, its social climate, its economy, and its perceived status on the world's stage.***

This material should be of immediate value to those teachers already in the classroom. Additionally,

- It should be of value to college students who think they are being prepared for entering the classroom.
- It should be a guide for supervisors, principals, and board members charged with evaluating and revitalizing the classroom experience.
- It will be enlightening to the millions of parents who know that something is wrong but haven't known how to help.
- It should be interesting to everyone; especially nonparent taxpayers, who want to help but have not known how.

It is evident by now that continual infusions of money do not ensure a better education.

- Higher salaries have not produced better test scores.
- New buildings, new technology, and more gadgets have not reduced dropout rates or encouraged more college entrants.
- Loud, publicized, frequently unreasonable threats to, by, and between unions and administrations have yielded results that rarely affect what goes on in the classroom.
- Rewritten dress codes and attendance policies have not changed students' attitudes toward attending or succeeding—and on and on it goes. You can list as many failed attempts as I.

Yet, these things are worshipped because they are familiar, easy to discuss at meetings, easy to understand, comfortable, *and perceived to be meaningful... perceived to be measurable... perceived to be remedial.* They are not!

If those things worked, we would have solved education's shortcomings years ago. It is time for a fresh understanding—be it ever so fundamental. Oftentimes there is a tendency to blame others for problems. Parents blame their kids; kids blame their teachers; teachers blame their school administrators; administrators blame their school board; colleges blame high schools; high schools blame junior high schools; junior high schools blame elementary schools; elementary schools blame their socioeconomic community; and communities blame their schools.

The unfortunate fact is that each of those accusations has a glimmer of truth. No matter where the fault lies, we—the literal owners of the school system and the activities that go on therein—must understand the classroom environment better. We must become familiar with the changes that will bring about its revitalization.

The existing cycle of behavior has to be broken! Surely, you have seen the futility, the frustration, the wasted energy, and the misplaced emotion as your cat aggressively chases its own tail. Education, as a profession, can chase its own tail no longer. That futility is exhausting. With exhaustion comes weakness; with weakness comes defeat.

> ***Using the results of standardized tests as a threat for funding reduction, promotions, demotions, terminations, and school closings, or for comparisons with other districts or other nations, borders on unethical. The practice is destructive!***

Tests ***do*** have a critical place in the day-to-day operation of a classroom. (We will discuss more about their proper use in Chapter II, "Tests and Measurements.") Until then, please recall the Hawthorne Effect from 1950, which clearly established that the very act of observing something changes its behavior. In this case, all the attention to standardized testing and the misuse of the results have changed the reality of classroom activities and teachers' behavior.

The costs of today's educational practices are not only measured in the misuse of billions of dollars, but are more critically measured by the coming generations, the children lost to a lifetime of unmet potential. Their inability to think critically, their having little respect for authority, for learning, topped by poor work habits and attitudes, will inevitably result in our continued decline. These unhappy, poorly educated, and mostly unproductive citizens will again mature, reproduce, and send *their* little five-year-old off to public school—and the cycle will start again.

Parents and tax-paying citizens without kids must also take a larger but carefully defined role in the education system that consumes the largest part of their property tax dollars. That system wastes their money and dramatically affects every aspect of their lives, yet few seem to notice. The public must understand why and how they need to step up and take an active role not only for the sake of the students but also for the good of the nation's economic health and security. The public must help us with the reinvigoration of what once was a superior social and economic world status. ***Without an educated populace, our system of government cannot (indeed, will not) survive.*** Without a well-informed public, supported by a free press and a just court, poor decisions will be made, and the press will become only a tool for mob titillation and propaganda. We must get to the place in our society in which every vote is based on a thoughtful decision by a well-informed public, or we cannot survive. Educating that public is what we must do.

If we continue the trend we have allowed to develop, the footsteps of millions of undereducated, unsophisticated, unaware youngsters will soon tread a path so narrow and so deep that only a catastrophe will shock us back to reality—if back we can ever come.

If we continue the trend that we have allowed to develop, we will have more families on public assistance than families paying taxes. There will be too few young brains to solve our many new problems; too few citizens capable of creating the new industries and businesses necessary to drive our economic recovery; and no way to generate the revenue required to fund the critical work of those who do make it in spite of the system.

This nation can only reimagine itself into what it once was with the support of an educated populace. There is no other way to successfully run a republic! Look around the world today where governance and reform is being tried by mobs. We, as a struggling nation, have been where they are several times before. Need we go there again, before we are shaken into our senses and realize how critical a quality education is for all?

Parents and interested taxpayers have for some time let their school board members, their school administrators, their classroom teachers, *and* their students know that they are fed up with the results. However, they have not told them exactly what they want done about it. Simply shouting "Fix it!" is not constructive leadership and will yield no reform. Revitalization requires a comprehensive, surgically specific approach.

…and the conductor shouts: ***"That sounds terrible…now play it again!"***

It is my hope that the ideas expressed in this book will give clear benchmarks against which one can measure how best our schools should serve our children and thereby our nation. It will offer fundamental methods for problem identification and will make clear a plan for the remediation of those identified problems.

The same concerned, informed public, which already pays for and therefore owns the school system, coupled with classroom teachers who carry the responsibility for "delivery," must become the motivating force that brings about a rapid revitalization. We do not—at least, not at this time—need to discuss most of the glitzy revisions being tried today. Voucher systems, storefront schools, magnet schools, charter schools, open enrollment, or more computers *are not* in themselves the answer. Please consider:

- To be concerned, even to become informed, is nothing without **action.**
- Action, as a commitment, is useless without it being focused on specific **assigned tasks.**
- Those tasks are equally meaningless unless they are executed in small, manageable, and **logically sequenced steps,** executed as methodically as if they were critical gears in a well-run machine, and understood as a unique part of the whole.

Who is going to do exactly what to whom?

Exactly when, where, how, and in what sequence?

When that is completed, who is going to do what with the evaluation of the results from the tests that were designed to measure success?

These questions need accountable names assigned to each: accountable individuals, capable of the art of teaching, reliable as subject-matter experts, dedicated, energetic, and well reimbursed.

When these few basic concepts are understood and implemented:

- Subject-matter expert teachers can be hired. (Who?)
- Comprehensive curriculum plans can be made. (What?)
- The effectiveness of the lesson (the delivery) can be honed. (How?)
- Delivery and retention can both be measured (evaluation/ diagnosis).

- Critical thinking will become commonplace. (Have we developed a nation of citizens capable of thinking things through to their ultimate conclusion, to the cause-and-effect relationships of any situation?)

Imagine a day in the future when we teach students how to read, write, and calculate as well as to understand their role in society. They will be able to understand cause-and-effect relationships; understand that the cop car they just torched or the flagpole they just tore down belonged to them. Through well-developed critical thinking, they will foresee the results of their every action, both as individuals and as managers of a renewed nation. Imagine a local pub where a conversation between a plumber and a politician sounds like a conversation between Hamilton and Jefferson, or a written proposal by a highly paid executive is delivered with the clarity, accuracy, and carefully worded poignancy of a Kennedy or a Clinton.

If we don't make these things happen, if we can't, or if we simply continue to look the other way, then in a very short time we will have contributed to the destruction of our culture. We will complete our deterioration to a much lesser-world status, will be owned and controlled by any one of several smarter, more energetic, and more disciplined societies. Why do we naïvely think we are too big and too special to fall? Has no one studied history?

The Revitalization of the American Classroom will help focus your concerns and will suggest to you possible methods of remediation. You should be able to take action on general concepts as well as specific tasks. This book will help you do so in understandable, achievable, and quite manageable pieces. We simply need a methodical and measurable approach toward bringing about such a "revitalization."

It all starts with your understanding, it grows with your action, and it succeeds with your relentless involvement. Repeatedly, you will hear me say:

"The Revitalization of the American Classroom is not a spectator sport."

Thomas R. Shipley, EdD
thomshipleybooks@hotmail.com
www.thomshipleybooks.com

About This Book

School is a common experience shared by everyone. Public or private, no matter the setting, school was and is an undeniable part of our collective experience. For better or for worse, it shaped us academically, socially, culturally, and, in almost every case, economically.

School is an experience we all remember and relate to, regardless of our age. We all have strong opinions on just how the classroom experience affected us and how it should have been conducted. We recall good teachers and bad teachers. We complained as students; we complain as adults. We complain as employers; we complain as taxpayers. Education can easily be one of the most expensive, complained-about endeavors our society has ever attempted.

This book is directly intended for all current teachers, teachers-in-training, parents, and taxpayers who would like to take action to correct some of the traditional complaints about school. It contains a set of ideas that are specific enough to be implemented in your local classroom, and yet broad enough to be raised like a large umbrella over the entire education system in your district.

This is not a research document. It is an anecdotal record of many observations and conclusions. It is based on personal experiences and challenges. The ideas are, on the other hand, *not* emotional, opinionated short stories. Every page is an effort to share with interested readers my observations of what goes on in the American classroom; it is an effort to share the philosophies and proven techniques I have acquired.

The ideas expressed in this book started in 1967 as essays to my school's principal. It was my first year out of the classroom, and I was embarrassed and appalled at what I was seeing from my new perch as an administrator. As my new boss—try after try—rejected my attempts to improve the environment in "his" classrooms, I started to file my observations and ideas. When I retired in the late 1970s, I updated and tried to publish these ideas. Again, I was rejected, this time by publishers. In defeat, I put publishing out of my mind. By the time I retired again in 2012, I had become familiar with (and successfully used) new techniques of self-publishing. Observing through my children, grandchildren, friends, and neighbors that the same problems still exist, and still thinking that I have something to offer, I decided to brush the dust off the yellowing pages, refresh my classroom observations, and publish my ideas at my own expense.

I am fortunate enough to have lived through one of the most interesting, invigorating, and fast-moving periods in American history. I learned from a wonderful childhood, from unusually great parents, from an above-average education, and from a career that spanned teaching in a county elementary school classroom to advising US congressional education subcommittees.

Not every generation is shaped by depressions, world wars, and international skirmishes beyond count, moon landings, sexual, moral, and cultural revolutions, integration, and technical advances beyond Buck Rogers's wildest imagination. We have come from a time in which children were sent to a different room while the adults discussed the movie *Gone with the Wind* to a time in which vaginal lubricants for postmenopausal women are advertised on national TV during breakfast. I have attended same-sex weddings;

encountered adults who don't know what an iron lung is; and worked with children who don't know what an ironing board is.

At 80, I rarely speak to anyone who remembers growing up without heat or running water, or carrying three spare tires for a Sunday drive. I often reflect upon the vast changes and improvements in the life around me. I appreciate—beyond words—how and why we got where we are, and I ponder where we are heading.

The art of observation and the skill of understanding cause-and-effect behavior have served me well. Those observations are offered here for your consideration and evaluation. We will discuss such topics as:

- Are teachers adequately trained?
- Are teachers adequately paid?
- Isn't teaching an easy job? (Short days, summers off…)
- Are standards being lowered to accommodate a mediocre student population?
- What does "teaching to the test" mean?
- Do we really know how to test for proficiency?
- How does one "teach"?
- How does one "learn"?
- How does one evaluate a competent teacher?
- How does one evaluate a successful student?

With the glaring ramifications of failure now blatantly evident despite decades of perceived "progress" at huge expense, it is frightening that we still don't seem to know the answers to these questions.

Can you have a meaningful discussion with your family (or even with your coworker) about what is the difference between students learning "data," "information," "knowledge," or "wisdom"? Do we even understand the distinctions or why that's an important conversation to have?

It seems to me that we have come to a place where a serious, intellectual discussion with the family or a small group of friends is embarrassing. Is it a lost art? Have you noticed the shallowness of a conversation when three or four couples get together? Discussing the salary of a football player is OK, even the revenue from the third sequel of some sci-fi movie, but what about "education," its costs and all of its ramifications?

Similarly, have you had any discussions recently about what jobs are taking talented young people away from teaching as a profession? Do you even know what the starting salary for a teacher in your district is? Do you know that in some states a first-year teacher working sixty hours per week for ten months would earn thirteen dollars an hour? Do you know what your state's per-pupil expenditure is?

These more critical conversations must no longer be avoided. These conversations must be based on facts and experiences, rather that emotions and hearsay. These conversations are directly related to your child's success in school.

Somehow, after years of trying, and after millions of dollars being invested, the professionals and bureaucrats have been unable to perfect our education system. By some standards, other (even poorer) nations have already passed us by. *Note:* Be careful. I have observed that quotes about international outcomes and comparisons are frequently based on questionable sample-size populations and on debatable variables of the population being tested. Do your homework before emotionally repeating a reported finding. Be sure they are comparing apples to apples—not generic group to an unrelated clutch of kids—based on a single variable.

While debatable to some, is it conceivable that the current deplorable conditions of the US government are based on our poor education system—on our citizens' inability to select competent representatives. Do our graduates (the voting public) understand the importance of and the process for selecting qualified candidates and weeding out weak and ineffectual elected officials, spotting corruption, or evaluating patterns of bad judgment?

Before we go further, just think for a minute:

- Is that kind of wisdom measured by standardized math or science test scores?
- Do we have the time and talent to teach critical thinking skills while concurrently being able to bring up our math and science scores?
- Which scores matter most, critical thinking or science?
- Is there a relationship between the two?
- Are test scores of any value without the wisdom of how to use them for good?

Our nation's government is (by design) not the simple democratic form in which we can choose to vote on every question and every line item in a budget. As a republic, we vote for representatives who are expected to best represent our needs and efficiently run the government for us. This concept was intended to prevent the passage of legislation during times of high emotion and mob control. This was the founding fathers' attempt to protect the informed minority from an uninformed majority. There are many examples in which it has worked well. Remember that not so long ago the majority thought that blacks and whites should not serve together in the military; that being gay was a mental illness; and that women should not vote. Always be cautious about the wisdom of the uninformed majority.

The selection of these capable representatives requires an educated public capable of critically thinking through all the qualifications of a candidate and the ramifications of placing their vote. If there is one serious indictment against our education system, it is that we teach our children how to read and write and count, but not how to think critically. Critical thinking is required just as much to evaluate and select capable candidates to represent our needs and philosophies, as it is to design our satellites, cure our ills, and manage our households and relationships.

We have understandably become so dependent on the demands of a two-income family that to take on such a major topic as the revitalization of our public schools would be very inconvenient, time-consuming, and (*perceived to be*) expensive—a real infringement on our twenty-first-century lifestyle. We give lip service to the criticality of an improved education system, much as we do to global warming and air pollution. *Addressing these critical— in some cases lethal—problems would indeed be time-consuming. We as a society and we as individuals are convinced that we have "so many more important things to do, we'll just let our leaders take care of everything for us. Besides, what are we paying them for?"*

"The Congress is running the government and the educators are running the school system." Are these the same individuals on whom we spent so much time evaluating before choosing? Have you ever had a class in which you discussed the need for, the how to, the skills required for selecting a qualified candidate? Probably not—and yet our system of governance totally depends on the citizen voter knowing and performing that civic duty. I once heard a woman in my neighborhood say, "I'm voting for Kennedy. He's Catholic and he's handsome. What else do I need to know?"

Parents and tax-paying citizens must take a more active role in their education system; an active role not only for the sake of the students, but also for the good of the nation. In most cases, we know that informed and educated parents raise smarter, well-rounded kids who are in turn more successful. Notice, I suggested "informed" parents, not "involved" parents. Chapter V will discuss the difference in detail.

It is not difficult to observe that:

- parents who started reading to their children at infancy,
- parents who regularly discuss today's news and politics at the dinner table,
- parents who discuss the reasons for and value of an education (be it academic or technical),
- parents who discuss and explain social and cultural values, personal obligations, manners, and dress codes as being the student's individual responsibility to their future success and happiness, produce smarter, better-behaved, more financially successful, well-adjusted, employable kids.

One-on-one parental involvement **with the child** is key. Involvement **with the school**, the team, or the PTA, is complementary. When you see students standing around with their mouths hanging open, with their pants down below their butt, with their hats on backward at the lunch table, with audio buds in their ears during class, with no pad and pen available for any class, and texting during a lecture—know that none of these things will be corrected by parental involvement with the PTA bake sale or by carpooling for the ball team. We have known several basic facts for years. It is not a news flash that better-behaved, better-dressed, more-articulate, socially adjusted kids get better jobs, make better decisions, earn better salaries, and become better leaders. The trick is in understanding how parents should be involved (Chapter V) with their children's education to assure these characteristics.*

The ideas expressed in this book will give you clear benchmarks against which you can measure the relevance of your school's performance, the efficiency of your teachers, the academic growth of your students, and a few suggestions for parents. It will give you methods for problem identification and will make clear a plan for the solution of those problems. A concerned, informed public, which is already paying dearly for their school system, should be more concerned about its investment. That same public would not support a theater in which every play was performed badly, or rehire a painter who slopped paint on their carpet—and yet all they do about education is complain—while continuing to pay the bill.

We simply need a methodic, commonsense, tested approach toward bringing about "Classroom Revitalization." I believe you will find that fundamental approach within the following chapters. You will be offered several actions and specific tasks necessary to realize a revitalization. Those concepts are offered in understandable, manageable, and achievable pieces, requiring no additional costs.

Somehow, we must find the time and energy to roll up our proverbial sleeves, pump up our sagging attitudes, and, using this newfound knowledge, get to work. *It's knowledge when you know it—it's wisdom when you know how to use it.*

Are you reading to your children? Are your children reading to you? Are you volunteering to read to local preschool children? Are you regularly sharing intelligent, important conversations with your children? Is there a world globe in your family room? Do your kids understand where US soldiers died today? Do they know how many women and children were displaced yesterday and what that really means? Have you ever discussed the family budget? Alternatively, are your children being raised by the violent TV or computer screen out of sight in the next room, so you can get on with the important "stuff" that keeps you so busy?

There is nothing about *The Revitalization of the American Classroom* that is a spectator sport.

---

* *It would be wonderful if every student, teacher, and parent could read the very short, true story titled "Lang Lang." It is a short book and a quick and easy read. It details the level of sacrifice Lang Lang's parents were willing to make, and the commitment to him they were willing to give, to develop his skills as a young pianist. It is admittedly not very practical—but it makes an impressive point, demonstrating the results of such parental commitment. You will quickly see that they did not **teach** him piano—they **supported** his education. Please try to find time to listen to him play, and then you determine if it was all worth his parents' sacrifices.*

Acknowledgments

I am sure that each reader fully realizes how many times a manuscript must be read and reread, edited and corrected—even individual words and punctuations argued over and debated.

For his time, patience, kindness, wisdom, and talent in making hours of edits, I am indebted to my partner, Chris Taylor. Thanks, Chris.

For her insight—gained through teaching experience—and wisdom applied to classroom success, I send sincere appreciation to my longtime friend and peer, Patricia King Swanson. Thanks, Pat.

The Importance of Experience

The chances are very good that you have never had to wear a pair of your big brother's outgrown shoes to school. It may be difficult for you to imagine how it feels to a little boy in the fourth grade to be aware of his shoes with every step; to be aware of his shoes while he is expected to be thinking about arithmetic. You probably never gave much thought to the depth of his embarrassment, his aggravation, or the discomfort of those hand-me-down shoes as they grind away, wearing a hole in the heel of his raggedy socks.

This little fellow has an overpowering desire to remain inconspicuous; a desire not to let anyone know just how much misery he is in...just how poor he really is...or how much he'd love to have shoes and socks that were his, that fit, and that were comfortable.

Only the shaggy cat curled up in the corner of his kitchen knows for sure what else goes on in this child's house. What is it that daily shapes his every thought and action? Is there enough food to go around? Is there enough love to go around? Is there time for anyone to read aloud to him, build a birdhouse, and teach him to make scrambled eggs? Has he ever been to a museum? Are manners, posture, dress, and social behavior a part of his everyday conversations? Has anyone ever said, "Don't talk with your mouth full," "Did I hear you say 'Thank you'?" or "Honey, how'd it go in school today?" Does anyone really care?

Even worse, are we sure that this boy's parents have the personal background, experiences, and understandings that *they* need to offer him these social graces or these life skills, much less any academic help?

Kids from Appalachia to the cities and from blue-collar neighborhoods to gated golf-course communities all have daily experiences about which we, as their teachers, rarely think. Those experiences *can't* be the same for any two youngsters. Yet—for good and bad—we treat all students in a classroom similarly, expecting each child to fit into some preconceived mold. Do we ever consider that the experiences students bring with them may not have any relevance to the lesson that we plan to teach today?

There are some educators who go so far as to say that they don't want to know about their students' home life. They boast that they treat all of their students alike and have an air of pride in proclaiming that philosophy. On the surface, this sounds noble and honorable—as indeed it is intended to be. The problem is that educating children is a personal and complex endeavor, and the individuality of students, what has shaped them, what influences them every day, what environment they go home to, and all of their past experiences work together to make up who they are. Everything *they* say and everything *they* do is based on the sum total of experiences, and these experiences must not be overlooked—not by accident and not on purpose. Everything *we* say and everything *we* do is translated and interpreted by them through their accumulated experiences.

One very unfortunate but very common misconception is that of mistaking the absence of experience with the absence of intelligence. *It is not!* If you pay close attention, you will observe that not only educators are guilty of this misconception. We can see it in our coworkers and neighbors, saying or doing what we see as stupid things only because they have no experiences by which to measure the immediate situation.

As difficult as it may be to believe, I would like to give you an example. This is only one of many true, eye-opening experiences.

A graduate assistant and I walked past the grand opening of a new ice-cream shop on a main street in Washington, DC. I offered to treat each of us to an ice-cream cone—on our way to our next congressional visit.

"Oh, no thank you. They are far too messy!"

I laughed it off, and insisted that we support the new shop. I purchased two very small single-dip cones of vanilla. To my absolute horror and surprise, within the next few steps I saw ice cream running down the hand of this well-dressed, academically brilliant doctoral student as he ate away at the side of the cone that was facing him, while leaving the sun to melt the sides not readily accessible to his mouth.

Not once did he turn the cone to lick the other melting sides or even try to solve the problem of the inevitability of the melting ice cream. It was rapidly becoming, just as he had feared, a big mess.

After recovering from this potentially embarrassing situation, we discussed my observation that he didn't know how to attack an ice-cream cone...a skill I mistakenly thought to be as involuntary as breathing. He explained that his very busy, professional, high DC-society parents had never allowed any of the children to have an ice-cream cone because it might mess up their clothes. As I went on as if I were teaching a graduate class, he absorbed the idea of turning the cone and licking the delicious melting dribbles on the other side.

We must be sure that our assumptions, the words we use, the situations we refer to, the places and things that we take for granted—even sarcasm, jokes, and innuendo—are all relevant to the audience. *Relevance comes from experience.* If we don't take the time and effort to recognize this, a student's internalization of what we are trying to teach may well be lost. I once had a young deaf student ask me, "Why would anyone keep their cat in a bag?"

From the little you read about our young student with his big brother's outgrown shoes, you can glean enough information to turn words into images and images into an understandable situation. You can feel enough of the emotion to put yourself into that youngster's shoes.

> *As an effective teacher, you must—one way or another, actually or vicariously—always bring your students' experiences up to a level where they understand the situation you are about to present __and__ always offer relatable experiences that will enable them to understand and absorb what you are about to teach. You have a responsibility to be sure they have the depth of understanding (both in concept and vocabulary) needed to relate to and internalize your upcoming lesson.*

You must continually ask yourself, "Do these students have the experiences they need to understand the words, names, places, or concepts I am about to use in my lesson? Do their experiences allow them the luxury of fully engaging in the thought process to internalize ideas based on *my* assumption that they know the things, words, places, and names of people that I am about to use?"

If not, you are doing your students a disservice by not offering them these missing experiences; experiences to which they may have had no exposure. You must find a way to give them the foundation, the base from which the upcoming lesson may be related and absorbed. Without this effort, the damage may well be irrevocable. Since education is a complicated web of interrelated pieces, each building on the other, there can be no weak blocks or missing pieces.

Why would I fear a cannon or fully understand your conversation about the famous battle of 1812 if I don't know what a cannon looks like, what it does, what it sounds like, and what its role has been throughout history? Not all students are within a day trip to Fort McHenry. This is what I continually refer to as "actually or vicariously." In the absence of a trip, you must give your class the image of and the importance of a cannon before proceeding. You must create the missing experience.

How can I imagine the difficulties in settling the West if I don't know where "the West" is, what a Conestoga wagon is, how and why oxen are involved, or even what an ox is? I probably have no reference point as to how difficult it would be to walk thousands of miles over mountains and desert. Do I even know what a desert is, or what a mountain range is, or why crossing either might be a problem? "Why couldn't they just go around another way?" or "Why didn't they take a train?" or better yet, "Why don't they just buy a farm near here?" Obvious? Not without a past story, picture, or experiences to which one can make a reasonable reference.

> *As your student, my ability to assimilate what you are about to teach me is inexplicably related to my understanding of the words you are about to use and the things and events to which you are about to refer.*

If you haven't had an experience exactly like the hand-me-down shoes, or at least one very closely related to it, the scenario might seem more humorous than uncomfortably real. While you may be able to envision something from the text, your degree of understanding, your sympathy, your relationship to, and your internalization of the situation are not as solid as someone who has had a similar experience. Allow me to reemphasize: *the depth and breadth of one's understanding is directly and undeniably related to one having the combination of previous experiences that enable your presentation to be understood.* Before you start your presentation, it is up to you to establish "Where is each student?" and "What should he or she know to better internalize/comprehend what I'm about to say?"

Fortunately for us all (students and teachers), most situations do not have to be experienced firsthand, in real time. In the hands of a skilled teacher or concerned parent, they may be presented vicariously. The situation may be contrived or real, a comparative demonstration, or simply a picture, a story, an experiment, or any simulated experience. **Understanding this and recognizing it— being able to step up to the plate with a story, an example, or a picture when you see that a needed experience is missing—is one of the many skills that separate an educator from an instructor, a teacher from a lecturer.**

Ask yourself:

- "Am I an expert in my field?" (especially if you are a beginning, inexperienced teacher).
  There is nothing more important than being the subject-matter expert. You cannot fake being a good teacher; you cannot be respected as an authority unless you know your subject.
- "Can I be an actor, a storyteller, a poet, a friend, a mentor, a role model, a counselor, and a disciplinarian all at the same time?"
- "Am I willing to spend several hours in preparation for each hour in class?" (Believe it!)
- "Do I have the skill to evaluate where each student is, and understand how to move them forward?"

- "Will I be able to continually observe my students' behavior?" Asking repeatedly, "Is this working? Is this holding their attention? Are they getting my points?" Not, "Am I getting through the required curriculum on schedule?"

Every student comes to you with a different level of life experiences, and these experiences weave the basket in which each will carry your lesson.

Vicarious experiences will usually suffice, especially if presented by a skilled storyteller, which is to say a good teacher. It is not necessary for a small child to burn her hand on the stove to understand the potential danger of that thing lurking in the kitchen. On the other hand, every parent has the responsibility to provide this education through examples, explanations, and serious stories, making the undesirable experience of a serious burn as real and as relevant as possible. The criticality of that vicarious lesson seems elementary and obvious, yet you cannot imagine the parent waiting until the child burns herself to teach that lesson. The impact of the experience need only be supported by a very few words, carefully making a comparison, establishing a cause-and-effect relationship. Failing to expose the child to this blunt reality is not only negligent, it is extremely self-defeating.

News on the TV, events in the neighborhood, and conversations at the breakfast table are all opportunities to expand a child's experiences. Each experience becomes a building block toward his or her eventual wisdom. *Protecting children from the realities of life only makes the adult involved feel better for that warm and fuzzy moment. It rarely supports the growth of the child.*

Here is where we start to teach one of the most critical lessons of all: *cause-and-effect relationships.* From algebra to zoology, there is a reason why things are as they are. Every one of us has at times grown tired of a child repeatedly asking, "Why?" Not to capitalize on this inquisitive nature and enthusiasm is a serious mistake made frequently. Answering "Why?" is the beginning of building a library of experiences that will serve the student throughout his or her life.

At first, you may have the tendency to answers all students' questions by stating, "It's the rule." You may have a desire to try discipline over education, as in, "Because I said so." Please understand, and try not to forget, that the question itself is a sign that students can go no further in the building process until you assist with *placing this one piece of the puzzle* into its proper position. Not just where it fits, but how and why it goes there. When a student's life experiences do not include anything that allow him or her to internalize the idea you just presented, it's likely this question will be missed on your next quiz. Such children will start down the path of being labeled as "not good learners" or "not paying attention," when in fact all that is needed is a few words of understanding as to the *process* or the *how* or the *why*.

With the time and personal attention you spend on the question, you enable this lesson to be internalized. Once the question is resolved and the thinking process is understood, practiced, reinforced, and honed, feelings of pride and success will engulf the student. Each of these little moments of success will breed the desire for another feeling of success, and the enjoyment of the thinking process will grow slowly but surely into an *involuntary response.*

The life skills of "cause-and-effect," "action and consequences," and "process and product" must start at infancy. They must be presented in short, simple, understandable segments. In due time the subject matter will change—the vocabulary will change—but the criticality of understanding and applying the yin and yang remains the same. Even free play is a learning experience in cause-and-effect living. Could the consequence of not being picked for the team be a constructive life skill? Could "**not** winning a ribbon at the school fair" be a building block in character?

Always remember that an effective teacher must simulate within the classroom those experiences necessary to facilitate the students getting maximum meaning from a lesson. A great teacher will find those experiences within the child, within the class, or within the children's immediate environment, and then use them *before* proceeding with the lesson. *The need for such explanations can easily be identified and therefore anticipated during lesson planning.* They will fall out effortlessly during the preparation of the final exam. (This concept, the value of preplanning, and the reason for the early design of your measurement tools is covered in detail in Chapter II, "Tests and Measurements.") The need for stories, props, or guest speakers will become obvious during your advance planning.

This preplanning detail is, in itself, one of the fundamental activities that will help you grow in gaining *wisdom over technique.* There is a conspicuous and undeniable difference between a maestro and a drum major.

One of the most critical of all lessons for every student to learn in every subject area is cause-and-effect relationships. Do they understand the actual (or implied) connection between related activities? Between related processes? Can they draw the correct conclusions from an observed or described action, and predict the probable outcome?

> *To tell a new violin student where to place her left elbow is a rule, and you are her instructor.*
> *To explain the reason for the placement of her left elbow— the cause and effect, the result of proper posture—is an education, and you are her teacher.*

No matter what the subject, we must (within as many lessons as possible) try to work in:

- critical thinking and reasoning
- sequential processing
- cause-and-effect relationships
- attitudes toward relevance/usefulness of the assignments
- social and behavioral obligations and responsibilities
- understanding of the need for immediate and lifelong learning
- *and* the 3 Rs.

Somehow, the teacher must make the lesson relevant to this child's life today or in the imaginable future. The complaint of "irrelevance," second only to "presentation," is a frequent criticism. Is it that the subject is truly irrelevant, or could it be that it has not been presented in a sufficient framework of its relationship to upcoming experiences? The question becomes, "Are you instructing a topic, or are you teaching a child?"

I am reluctant to admit how frequently embarrassed I am about my level of knowledge of geography and history. I took and passed every class that was required, but didn't know how little I knew until I became a citizen of the world. As an educator, I now see how exciting, interesting, and—in some cases—entertaining geography and history can be. I have also observed, with a heavy heart, how frequently these critical subjects are taught so poorly.

Some youngsters may have lots of information from memorizing facts, but do not have the wisdom to apply them. Wisdom is not the regurgitation of data, or even the parroting of information on a test. The responsibility of every teacher is to provide (or take advantage of existing) experiences and information as a first step, and then to add to and guide the child to develop the experience, turning data into information, information into knowledge, and knowledge into wisdom.

1. **Data:** A young person sees a tool. The tool has a handle and a blade with teeth on it. It resembles a tool he or she knows is called a "saw." One can be seen hanging on a rack nearby.
2. **Information**: A parent tells the person that that is a coping saw.
3. **Knowledge**: A carpenter tells the person it is for slowly cutting curves and fancy cuts on small- to medium-sized boards.
4. **Wisdom:** A young person is given a piece of wood with a curved line drawn on it, is shown how to hold the saw, follow the line, and (in due time) successfully uses the coping saw as intended.

The child has progressed from seeing "a thing" to learning "its name," to understanding "how it works," to perfecting the skills of "using" what has been learned. Ultimately, wisdom is not only knowing how to use something, it is knowing when and where not to use it.

If the next day, absent any supervision, the youngster attempts to cut the end from an oak 4x4 post, he or she would have serious trouble. It would indicate that the child had not yet gained the wisdom we had hoped for. If schooled in the thought process of cause-and-effect thinking by a good teacher, the problems experienced while trying to cut the larger and harder board could be used to recall the experience they were warned about (but forgot) when told "small- to medium-sized boards." This thought process and additional experience, coupled with all the youngster has now been exposed to, leads him or her closer to the wisdom of properly using a coping saw. This is wisdom through guided, enhanced experiences.

Always keep in mind that, above all, your job is turning data into information, information into knowledge, and knowledge into wisdom. Ask yourself repeatedly:

- Can your students think through a situation—be it math or music—and come out with a better understanding than when they entered it?
- Do they possess and know how to use the physical and/or mental tools they need to complete the task?
- Can they evaluate a situation and think through what steps will get them to a satisfactory solution?
- Can they evaluate, prioritize, and anticipate various possible outcomes?
- Do they understand the necessity for and appropriate place for negotiation and compromise over strict adherence to process?

You must always be alert to observe the cause-and-effect activities of each child and of each lesson. "What triggered what?" must never be far from your observation of the students' classroom behavior. Otherwise, you are simply going through the motions, without being aware of the effectiveness of your style and process.

Each teacher must customize and personalize the practice of observation. An art teacher—teaching the effects of a light source on the shadow of a vase—will use this skill differently than a European geography teacher. Yet, each must be aware of the fundamental experiences (or lack of experiences) that students have brought with them to this lesson.

If I were to ask you to "Go out to my workshop and bring me a rasp, a brace, a keyhole saw, and a half-inch expansion bit," would your experience allow you to complete this very basic request? This task seems to me to be a perfectly reasonable request for tools I will need to complete a specific job.

To one of *my* kids, having been raised on a farm and involved with an active, operating workshop, it would have been executed quickly, easily, and without error. The task was clearly stated, understandable, and achievable; the words all had immediate and relevant meaning **based on their experiences.**

On the other hand, if I had asked one of my visiting nephews—all of whom are intelligent, successful athletes and all-around good students and great guys, but raised by a busy professional dad in a city house without a workshop—the request would have been threatening, unachievable, embarrassing, frustrating, and totally nonproductive. These feelings yield to self-defensive behavior and rebellion, and can quickly lead to an absolutely avoidable and unnecessary behavior problem.

That difference in attitude, behavior, and outcome would have been based **not on intelligence,** but on **experience.** Confucius said, "The beginning of wisdom is to call things by their proper name." Wisdom can never be achieved without understanding not only the proper name, but also what it does, why it works, and how it fits with other related things. Knowing that proper name, understanding what it does, how it does it, and how it relates to other things all come from experience. Experience is mostly gained by "doing" classroom exercises, teacher's examples, homework, group projects, etc. Here too, as in so many areas, volume/quantity is not important. Your careful design of the exercise is key to maximizing a student's ability to comprehend and internalize the concept.

Nearly any child growing up in the city, in any home without a workshop, would be incapable of completing many tasks that are second nature to farm kids; just as incapable as a child raised on a farm would have been if he were told to perform tasks that city kids perform with ease every day.

These children are not stupid, not inattentive, not lazy, nor disrespectful. They are suffering from the same things that students face daily in the classroom: *The lesson being presented is*

not in harmony with their experience. Put another way, the following things do not point to lack of intelligence, but simply to lack of experience:

- An inability of your students to assimilate words into images or concepts; their inability to internalize the lesson without a clear reference point.
- A teacher's premature commencement of the instruction process without considering students' possible lack of experiences.

For years I have heard music teachers preach, "Practice makes perfect." That is not so! Repeating the same mistake one thousand times will ingrain that mistake into your intellectual and kinetic being. "Perfect practice," on the other hand, goes a long way toward making the performance more perfect.

Consider this. The reason most deaf people cannot articulate speech clearly is because they have never heard—experienced—articulate speech. Never in the twenty-first century would you consider that their throat is anatomically missing a part or they lack the intelligence to speak. When signing to a deaf person, the sign you use is often difficult to interpret unless the context of the conversation is established in the mind of the receiving person. You give the sign (the word) an "experiential" context. For example, had I just returned from an overseas trip to Poland and finger spell "P-O-L-I-S-H" to my deaf friend, he would understand I was referring to a country. On the other hand, if I were to point at my feet, frown, and finger spell "P-O-L-I-S-H," my deaf friend would understand I was referring to my scuffed shoes. Without having established a context, the conversation would have been confusing. Likewise, the learning process is at its best when the lesson to be learned is taught by an informed subject-matter expert and placed in a meaningful context.

Calling something by its proper name is a simple, basic skill. It begins the process previously discussed of moving from data to information, information to knowledge, and knowledge to wisdom. This is a basic beginning platform for learning—very rarely discussed in the teacher's lounge of your local school. We all have moved from knowing our numbers to arithmetic, from arithmetic to balancing our checkbook. Neither of those skills proves we have any financial wisdom. We have all gone from learning our alphabet to spelling words; from spelling words to making sentences; from reading sentences to understanding the meaning of the groupings of words. Yet, some well-paid executives cannot write coherent, well-thought-out memos. The assembly of and use of all those skills (data, information, knowledge) are all pieces of the process toward achieving wisdom. They are important, but they are a means to an end. Wisdom should be the end. On which do you think students are tested?

- DATA is just stuff. Does "1492" mean anything to you? Does "9/11"? How about "WWII"? Sure they do. You can snap back, "In 1492 Columbus discovered America." The problem is, that is false, that is shallow (even if it were true), and your life is no better off because you know this incorrectly taught "data." Imagine the lesson you could build around the question, "What was going on in 1491 that inspired Columbus's venture in 1492?" and "Why would the Queen of Spain fund such a venture?" Alternatively, "How many underlying reasons can we discover for the cause of the 9/11 catastrophe?" In a properly presented lesson, the dates would be learned vicariously, ***as a byproduct*** rather than a cause célèbre, and certainly never used as a test item to measure one's wisdom.

Data: A little boy can read the numerals "9-1-1."

- INFORMATION is an accumulation of stuff, rules, things, data, names, numbers, and facts. Information is the "what" of any situation. It is relatively narrow, often unrelated, and frequently meaningless *when standing alone.* Information is learned by repetitious use; that is, memorized. Frequently, children with natural wisdom and insight are judged as failures because they see no relevance in remembering and parroting back facts. In some, their basic intellect allows them to quickly see the bigger picture, the conclusion of the logic flow, without memorizing all the details. This can be both a blessing and a curse. Sometimes information can be critical, and sometimes blatantly irrelevant. Understanding that difference continues the growth toward knowledge. You, as the classroom teacher, as the ever-vigilant observer, must be constantly aware of the difference.

Information: The little boy knows how to call "911."

- KNOWLEDGE should follow the learning of appropriately grouped, related, sequenced, and focused information. It involves an awareness and understanding of the processing of the *use* of data and the *use* of information. Knowledge comprehends interrelationships and sequencing of facts. Knowledge is the "how" of any situation.

Knowledge: The little boy knows to call "911" when there is an emergency.

- WISDOM, the threshold across which masses have not yet tread. It can only mature with time and proper grooming. *It is rarely achieved without many life experiences and frequent, focused guidance from an experienced, wise, and caring mentor as a role model.* Wisdom is the "why" of any situation. It combines the ability to analyze, to judge, to evaluate, to prioritize, and to understand cause-and-effect relationships and accurately predict outcomes. It enables us to anticipate results when presented with "What if...?" It is the ultimate conclusion to and the use of data, information, and knowledge.

Wisdom: The boy saw his neighbor's house on fire and called "911."

Understand that had the boy called 911 because his goldfish died:

1. he would have learned the data (he knew the numerals 9 and 1), and
2. he would have learned some information (he knew that this particular combination of data meant something when put together), and
3. he would have learned the next level of knowledge (he knew that using this particular combinations of numbers on a phone would get help), but
4. he lacked wisdom. He had not progressed to critical thinking, to judgment, to consequences, to cause-and-effect results.

We are (as parents *and* teachers) very weak at teaching and measuring wisdom.

Notice how easy it is to measure points 1, 2, and 3. Imagine how difficult it would be to teach and measure point 4. What does your last exam look like?

Note: *Teachers must be able to offer all four of these levels of learning. Traditionally (previously), society was able to find a workplace for and absorb people who peaked out at every level. That is no longer true. Those* *whom we allow to get through without achieving wisdom may well be doomed to minimal employment at best. They will be unprepared for most modern workplace requirements. Jobs for the previously acceptable lower and even middle tiers are becoming less and less available. Even when they can be found, they are significantly less rewarding. We can no longer be content with providing workers for mills and industry. We must learn how to provide a citizenry skilled in thinking and communicating as well as doing.*

You will repeatedly hear my deep-rooted concern that there is a clear and pending danger that our representative form of government will not survive without an informed electorate. Added to that should be "an employee workforce." ***It is unthinkable that the safeguards our country's Founding Fathers intended—to prevent major legislation from being passed by the emotion of mob psychology—will be overpowered by an uninformed electorate.***

We as educators must never allow the majority to become uninformed voters. We can find many examples where uninformed mobs are easily controlled by malicious propaganda, resulting in death, destruction, and loss of civility.

Teaching is—in every way—a critically serious profession. It should only be performed by intelligent, well-educated, well-trained, dedicated, and energetic individuals.

In the classroom of a great teacher, every session can be an experience that is looked forward to, respected, enjoyed, and even fun. ***Success breeds pleasure, and pleasure wants to be repeated. Make the class interesting, valuable, and pleasant, and everyone will succeed; problems with discipline and attendance will slowly disappear.***

That same teacher has the responsibility to explain the life-relevance of the subject and how the lesson about to be studied will contribute toward one's life (not toward the passing of a standardized test). There can no longer be a "bottom of the class" as measured by traditional methods.

*The triangle player **and** the concertmaster must both perform flawlessly, or the entire audience will suffer.*

In the academic world, "C" students, especially those measured by previous test and measurement philosophies, are traditionally condemned. However, in real life, these students are frequently no less successful. Some who learn rapidly become bored while waiting for the lockstep process to catch up to their level of understanding, hoping the lesson might again challenge or stimulate them. Some learn best by seeing, some by hearing, others by doing. You must be able to understand and adapt to all those individual needs *at the same time*. Even your quizzes and exams must be able to capture a student's comprehension via different methods of testing. If you are new to education, or unfamiliar with classroom activities, let me tell you emphatically that teaching is very hard work. As you work to perfect what you are doing, there is never enough time.

We have discussed the need for the teacher to provide some catching up before the planned lesson begins. Teachers should not just jump in because some approved curriculum guide directs them to. Teachers should never assume that the class is ready for a unit. This does not mean that new words or new concepts that are going to be introduced during the lesson should be discussed out of context, out of sequence, before the lesson begins. It does mean that every lesson must be set up.

I am reluctant to call the set-up exercise a pretest because the very word "test" conjures up negative connotations in some people. Nevertheless, that is exactly what it is: a pretest—an evaluation, a measurement to establish where we are. The exercise can be very light. In the hands of a creative teacher, it can be fun, even a game. It is not intended to provide a grade. Its purpose is to provide insight into the readiness of each student.

Imagine receiving a call from a friend who asks, "Can you tell me how to get to the Museum of Art?" Teacher or not, you could not answer that question without additional information.

You understand clearly that you could not yet start your lesson on "how to get to the museum." You would have to ask, "Where are you departing from?" followed by, "How are your traveling: on foot or by car, bus, or train?" You might also ask, "Have you ever gone there before by bus or train, and do you have any money?"

Are these questions a pretest? Well, yes! Is that a bad thing? Was that a waste of time? Could you have dared to proceed with an answer without knowing where your friend is in relation to the lesson you're about to deliver?

Very few realize the dedication, depth of skills, and amount of real work and focused time it takes to be a great teacher! Let's review:

- Above all, a teacher must become a master of the subjects for which he or she is responsible. Expertise will be recognized and respected by the students, and will reinforce everything that is said and done. Incompetence will be spotted in a minute.

- A teacher must understand the criticality and techniques of developing a lesson plan well before the first day the lesson is to be presented.

- A teacher must develop the skills to design meaningful measurement tools (a quiz, a test, an exam) and know how and when to use the results, as well as understand the critical role tests and measurements play in a successful classroom experience. (This is a topic I will cover in Chapter II.)

- A teacher must anticipate where the class is in relation to the lesson about to be taught, and must learn how to measure that via a pretest of some kind.

- A teacher must make such a complete analysis of the lesson to be taught, that he or she can identify what experiences and vocabulary may be needed for the class to comprehend all the points and nuances of the upcoming lesson. A teacher must identify in advance any supplies and materials needed to provide these experiences, and design quality measurement tools.

- A teacher must incorporate contrived, vicarious experiences into the setup before the lesson starts, and then reevaluate the flow and logic of the lesson for possible adjustments.
- A teacher must do the same type of diagnostic procedure that a medical doctor does before prescribing medications for a patient.
- A teacher must use tests and measurement tools to adjust his or her techniques, style, and procedures.
- A teacher must use the same tool to measure and evaluate the progress and unique styles of each student.
- A teacher must understand test scores as a measure of one's ability to teach as well as—if not more than—the students' ability to learn.

The set-up exercise demands that the entire unit be planned well in advance—thought through in detail and sequence, and assigned specific goals and related tasks. Ask yourself, "How is this student going to be better off after this unit then he or she was before it?" Then design the specific steps to get there. Only then can a teacher evaluate exactly what background a student must have to comprehend this upcoming unit on the front side or, just as important, know how to design the test (the evaluation instrument) for later use on the back side. If the teacher has not clearly identified the specifics of the lesson *in advance*, how can he or she work toward those goals? How can the teacher design the set-up lesson without knowing all of the individual pieces in detail and in sequence? What experiences should students have, and which ones are they missing?

How can a test (a measuring tool) be developed to measure the student's comprehension of the lesson unless exactly what is expected has been clearly identified in advance as being a significant, worthwhile goal? When all that has been clearly recognized and documented, then, and only then, can a lesson be carefully taught (presented).

To borrow a line from Chapter V, "Parental Involvement":

> At this point, a very brief statement can be prepared and sent home to the parents explaining the relevance of the upcoming lesson, the goal of the exercise, and several suggested ways the family might support or encourage the unit.

The fact that pieces of information, experiences, or vocabulary words identified by your pretest as missing must not be viewed negatively. These are not signs of bad behavior or academic slowness, but simply an absence of pieces of information— of building blocks that you have determined this student has not brought to this lesson—regardless of the reason. It is your responsibility **not to start the lesson** *until each student has been given all the pieces of information that you have determined as necessary, but missing.* This concept is so basic that it should be embarrassing to professional educators that it is ignored so often. Ignoring it is usually justified by the reply, "We simply don't have time," "We must stay on schedule," or more commonly, "The student should have learned that last year."

If a high school boy fails Chemistry 1 because he repeatedly can't comprehend the formula usage, even if he performs exceptionally well in the lab, he is usually given two options:

1. Drop out of this class and perhaps also the academic program, or
2. Take chemistry over (and over) again.

When a weakness is noticed by the teacher, parent, or student early in the academic year, why is the student condemned to sit through the class for the next nine months? It is clear that he is not going to succeed. Someone must intervene to stop the bleeding. Rarely is the energy taken to find out why the student is unable to comprehend the formulas, to fix that specific problem, and then to have him try again with a better-equipped background. There was conspicuously no pretest given to determine if this student should ever start Chem. I. Maybe a quick record check will show that his Algebra I grade was an F, but his Geometry I was an A. Do lab skills and geometry skills have any commonalities? Do the demands of chemistry and algebra have any similarities? Do we recognize a pattern of what's missing, where he's weak, and where he is strong? As soon as we shed some light on the problem, we can focus on the remediation of this high school boy's weak area and strengthen it. Simply repeating the class without this analysis is a foolish and expensive waste of time and energy.

When such weakness has been diagnosed, identified, and isolated, everyone involved is now obligated to do double duty remediation: the student, the teacher, the parents, and the budget. Rarely do we discuss the fact that the costs of a lifetime of public assistance, unemployment, or incarceration are far greater to taxpayers than the costs of remedial education or the smaller student/teacher ratios needed to bring every child up to an acceptable level of education. Immediate remediation must become a standard practice. The problems must be identified and fixed where and when they happen, not a decade later.

Stop the band rehearsal...
Find out who played an incorrect note...
Teach them the correct fingering...
Discuss the criticality of properly placing that note...

Proceed, observing the personal improvement, pride, satisfaction, and all-around enhancement of the group.

How fundamental is that?
How expensive is that?
Why would you do otherwise?
You cannot just move on.
You cannot just fail the kid.

If a little boy or girl asked Mom how to bake brownies and Mom rattled off a list of things to do and ingredients to use, the depth of the child's comprehension would be directly related to the child's experience. If Mom used the words "measuring spoons" and that meant something to our little friend, it would register. It would become an important link in the instruction process, and learning would have begun.

However, if the little boy or girl was new to cooking and had never seen or heard of measuring spoons, a visual image would be missing and a whole series of negative events might unfold. Mom, knowing her child's lack of familiarity with the term, would stop her recitation of the recipe and describe the size, shape, color, location, and use of measuring spoons. She would explain the difference between a "t-spoon" and a "T-spoon." After she finally established a physical and/or a mental image, Mom could branch back to the main idea. **Without this** (remedial) interruption, without this setup, the original explanation could be vague, meaningless, and probably lost. **With it**, the lesson can now continue with some hope for success. Alternatively…

The child, unfamiliar with measuring spoons, stopped to figure out the new term. The child understood the word "measuring" from Dad measuring his or her growing height on the wall from time to time, and surely knew what "spoons" were. In a moment, he or she therefore deduces that this meant some special kind of spoons that contain a specific amount. But then this child suddenly realizes that that thought process diverted attention away from Mom's ongoing instructions for a brief time.

Now, let's refocus on Mom, and discuss how she reacts.

- She either shares in her child's delight and accomplishment of having pulled together past pieces of data into new information, maybe even information into knowledge, and she graciously repeat the parts of the recitation her child had missed.

- Alternatively, she shouts at her child, "You're not paying attention" and says that she does not intend to repeat all those instructions. She tells her child, "Learn to pay attention" or, more commonly, "You're just not ready for this yet."

How many times each day do you think this latter reaction is used in the nation's homes and classrooms? How often do you think this has to be said before little girls or boys will no longer have the desire to ask, "Mom, how do you make brownies?" or "Mom, may I work with you in the kitchen?"

How frequently do we turn missing experiences into negative feelings about school and education?... About learning?... About the students themselves?

Two things could have happened:

1. The mother could have said, "I have a better idea! Why don't we bake brownies together and you watch this first time? I'll talk you through how much fun it is and we'll talk about all the things we'll need to use"—i.e., give him or her the experience that's missing. Or,

2. Our little friend, knowing that he or she hadn't done anything wrong, and growing tired of undeserved criticism, simply says, "Never mind, Mom, I'll just look at the TV for a while."

Did the youngster drop out or was he or she pushed out?

Too many similar situations go on in the American classroom every day.

- They are easily identifiable.
- They are easily solvable.
- They can be corrected (in most cases) by existing staff.
- They can be resolved within existing budgets.

They simply need the introduction of some very basic teaching concepts and tools presently being ignored by far too many teachers.

The one potentially irresolvable problem in this revitalization attempt is the unwillingness of parents, teachers, administrators, and teacher-training institutions to admit that they are the major part of the problem, and then for them to accept the responsibility for immediate change.

I have actually found situations where the classroom teacher understands these concepts and tries to practice them—only to be told by the administration that the class is "off schedule," or "standardized test are looming." I once worked with a supervisor of foreign languages who absurdly insisted that every classroom in the county be on the same lesson on the same day to assure that they all get through *her* curriculum within 180 days. If she made an unannounced visit to a teacher in any high school, the teacher was expected to be on the lesson she had scheduled from the county office.

As we presently observe America's schools, the classroom can become a mostly comfortable environment for the faculty. Since the educators of today are a mirror image of their educational experience, many are comfortable with it, tend to accept it, and perpetuate it. The students are often taught the way their teachers were taught—too frequently with the same sarcasm, the same attitudes, the same misplaced energies, the same techniques, authority, and emotions. The errors are caught up and compounded in a cycle of self-perpetuation. That cycle must be broken.

In order to untangle a badly tangled string, one of the most constructive steps is to find an end, or (depending on your attitude) a beginning. Educators have been fumbling with this classroom tangle for a long time, each grabbing at a different twist, with very little coordinated and sequential plans for correction. *Complicated fads are conceived, given fancy names, and tried on thousands of children, only to die a natural death after a year or two. They take with them the frustration and lost opportunities of uncountable children—not to mention billions of wasted dollars.* Above all, the horror washes over you when you dare to think about the repercussions of the unfathomable loss in human potential.

Education must no longer be measured by a student's *volume* or *speed* of data retrieval. That has been the traditional, easy way out. There are libraries and computers for data retrieval and memory banks beyond reason. The quality and relevance of the life available to the next generation of students is directly correlated to the *education* received. Education is now evolving into one's ability to think, deduce, relate, resolve, anticipate results, and excel at cause-and-effect relationships. Students must understand the consequences of their behavior, of their every activity—not only on themselves, but also on the community, the society, and the budget of the government that they will be paying for.

Do you think the long-range cost ramifications of replacing the fancy globe on a streetlight recently broken by some delinquent kid has ever been discussed in depth with a big-city class? Did that kid ever think that, in one way or another, I am breaking my own streetlight? Was that kid ever offered the understanding that his or her family would ultimately pay for its replacement? Did anyone ever suggest that the parks and recreation budget was cut and there can be no basketball court, because the cost of streetlight replacement has gotten so high? Education is not only about math and science!

- How is this measured on a standardized test?
- How does this relate to cause-and-effect thinking?
- How does this contribute to an educated populace?
- Would you know how to turn this situation into a meaningful lesson plan?

Certain skills and facts must always be developed, learned, and perhaps even memorized, just as in the past. Additionally, we must now teach broader concepts, attitudes, and understandings, as well as the ability to think and problem solve. Our questions must be:

1. Have we given the student the basic tools (skills) with which to resolve life's issues? (Unquestionably, the three Rs are where the gathering of data starts.)
2. Have we started them on the path to understanding the problem-solving process? Do they fully comprehend that every action has a consequence?
3. Have we taught the student how to group disjointed information (e.g., cat, purr, and happy) into some level of knowledge?
4. Have we demonstrated the stick-to-itiveness required to see a situation through to completion?
5. Have we shown the student how to prioritize, how to sequence activities to achieve a predefined goal when the desired outcome *is* known?

6. Have we shown the student how to prioritize, how to sequence activities to resolve a problem when the desired outcome is ***not*** known?

7. Do students understand the interrelationship of and the importance of their individual role and obligation to themselves, to their family, to their employer, and to their society?

8. Do they understand the value of an education, of lifelong learning? (This must include the importance of the trades, the arts, and service of all kinds.)

9. Have we learned how to make the learning process relevant and enjoyable? Do you personally smile when you recall the eighth grade? (It is natural to gravitate toward pleasurable tasks and avoid unpleasant or irrelevant experiences.)

10. Have we worked toward wisdom rather than parrot like repetition of data or information? (This is a depth of thinking too frequently missed.)

    - Can our students see cause-and-effect relationships?

    - Can they predict new results and anticipated consequences that they have never previously experienced?

    - Do they fully comprehend the connections between the family, friends, the job, and the community; between the individual and society; the physical and the emotional; the technical and the artistic?

If we can answer most of these questions positively, employers will do the rest. *The classroom cannot and must not try to include every possible "workplace" environment and occupational skill.* If a student can be provided with successful experiences in areas similar to these, he or she will succeed in college, the workplace, and in their social, family, and community environments.

School must not be expected to be the sole source for a child's moral and ethical values, for their patriotism, their vocational and intellectual development, their behavior, their nutrition, and their personality.

Poor instructional skills, irrelevant curriculum, naïve administration, irrational decisions, unjust punishment, sarcasm, unexplained demands, poor planning, and negative attitudes are visible to children in one teacher or another every day, and frequently again when children go home. This results in their developing negative attitudes toward school, adults, education, authority, and society. Negative attitudes are easy to introduce and foster in the mini-society within a classroom, but they may take years to correct outside the classroom—if ever.

In the following chapters, we will isolate several specific problems and offer solutions that are within the reach of students, teachers, administrators, parents, and the budget.

- *They are brief by design: Too many readers and publishers are impressed by volume.*
- *They are specific by design: Too many conversations end in flowery ambiguity.*
- *They are easy by their very nature: Too many people refuse to start a brick wall because they never realize how small and manageable it is to set just one brick at a time.*

Using the one-brick-at-a-time approach, classrooms could realize a revitalization that is unequalled in simplicity and effectiveness. Not with multimillion-dollar computer networks; not with new gimmicks and course offerings; not with the infusion of megabucks—but simply by a change in the behavior pattern, techniques, and attitudes of our teachers, and with support by informed parents.

The only reference to monetary needs in this entire book will be my continual plea to shrink class size in the lower grades. While some voices claim that the pupil/teacher ratio is not significant, almost nothing we do to revitalize behavior will work when that ratio is at 51 to 1 or 45 to 1. How can any individual attention be given with such a disproportionate ratio? All pupil/teacher ratios must be reasonably decided. In my high school band, I'd love 150 to 1; in my theory and composition class, I'd be at my best with ten. In my fifth-grade general education class, I'd love about fifteen or twenty at most. (Warning: Conversations about average class size are dangerously irrelevant. Always remember that those numbers are a single variable, and that is always dangerous.)

Many of our problems are directly related to, and are without doubt the fault of, some teachers. Please understand that those inadequacies are not malicious. ***Most are directly related to the fault of the teacher-training institutions that failed to prepare them.*** Still other problems are the fault of "the system," the "traditional bureaucracy." Overriding everything is the attitude and the understanding of the student toward the value of education. Here again, developing students' attitudes is a shared responsibility between the classroom teacher, the community, and the home environment. Without a healthy attitude for the need for an education, you are climbing a steep and slippery incline.

I have heard intelligent students make excellent evaluations of a teacher's classroom technique and offer constructive suggestions for improvement. These comments usually come from a nonconforming student to whom no one will ever listen. Those who conform easily also accept blindly. We should listen to some of the "war stories" our children have to tell about their classroom experiences. Don't just listen to exceptional or above-average students. Also, listen to the thoughts and comments of your everyday kids. Talk to them about teacher evaluation, talk about curriculum evaluation, talk about classroom improvements. Ask the students!

All of our problems are identifiable and solvable. In the following chapters, we will explore them candidly, spell out commonsense solutions, and show how to establish a much higher level of classroom success and accountability.

We cannot—we must not—ignore the criticality of, the timeliness of, the immediate need for this revitalization.

Without financial independence and social competence, the next generation will be—more than ever in our history—sucking at the financial teat of public service. It will be doing it even more than they are today, and doing it at the expense of a dwindling few. That pyramid will inevitably invert and collapse.

Without a smart, well-educated, informed citizenry, you have no pool of employees capable of representing your companies' needs for growth and prosperity. Without an *employed* population, you have no customers to consume your product or service. Without a *thinking* public, you have no hope of your government succeeding.

This is **your** problem.

All of these solutions can be implemented with "you" as the catalyst, you a parent, you an educator, you a student, or you as an interested (tax-paying) citizen. Do not cop out by saying this is not your problem, or you are not qualified to get involved. If you truly relate to the suggestions in this book, you have in fact become qualified. You are well aware that sometimes your $2,500 riding mower needs to be revitalized by a three-dollar spark plug. You can be the fresh, energetic spark that begins to revitalize this multibillion-dollar machine called education.

We all have one thing in common: school. As parents and taxpayers, these are now *your* schools. They are more than likely being paid for by the largest line item in your local budget, funded by a very large percentage of your property tax.

The difference between your comfort level when driving with a sixteen-year-old driver and a twenty-six-year-old driver is the ten years of experience. During those years, you anticipate a growth in skills. Each near-miss, each accident avoided, each observation of another driver's inabilities to maneuver a turn, plus sheer hours behind the wheel, all accumulated to help the driver grow from "operating by technique" to "driving with wisdom." That wisdom came from the honing of experiences, mentored over time.

Do not assume that each student who is new to you is experienced. Do not judge them on what they bring to your classroom. Measure them on how they grow under the experiences that you—as their mentor—give them. I urge you to think about how everything you do in the next hour is influenced by the experience you bring to whatever it is you are doing. Never underestimate the importance of experience.

"The only source of knowledge is experience."
–Albert Einstein

CHAPTER II

TESTS AND MEASUREMENTS

A hammer in the skilled hands of a sculptor is a creative tool. Used at times with gentle, even tender strokes of accuracy; at other times with strong, deliberately percussive strength. The proper use of this tool enables the sculptor to produce something lasting, sometimes bold, sometimes delicate, observable, meaningful, and long lasting.

That same hammer in the hands of a lunatic can be a weapon of brutal destruction. The improper use of this same tool can result in repercussions that are ruinous, meaningless, and equally long lasting.

Too often, we as educators are not sure how to use the tools that are available to us for the careful sculpting of young minds. These tools, intended for creativity, become tools of irreversible damage.

There is no better example of this indictment than the misuse of the dreaded documents called tests. Adding significant insult to this injury is the *misuse* of the resulting scores that these tests produce. Both of these—the tool and the use of the numbers they generate—*can* be and *must* be used as carefully as an artist uses a fine, natural-hair brush. We must learn to redirect their traditional use, and turn them into creative instruments.

Unless the results—test scores—are used for some objective evaluation of what's going on in the classroom, tests and their results are a waste of time and money.

- What's going on with the individual student taking the test?
- What's going on with the class learning this specific lesson? And most important:
- What's going on with the teacher who prepared the lesson and delivered its content?

Only then does the test become a tool.

In the hands of the average teacher (and far too many boards of education), tests and the numeric results they generate are being used as weapons. This misuse of what should be a diagnostic instrument—a tool—is naïvely brought on by two critical flaws in the system. Both are easy to fix (as are most of the flaws in our classrooms), and neither costs anything.

I. Teaching institutions should be ashamed of the depth and quality of the education they offer in the area of tests and measurements, especially to their undergraduate students. In most cases, new teachers will teach the way they were taught, and test the way they were tested.

Look back and try to remember your attitude toward a big test or a state-mandated series of standardized tests.

- Did you have a good feeling looking toward a meaningful experience?

- Did you sense a *constructive* nature to what you were about to do?
- Did your teacher ever even hint at the idea of your participating in a diagnostic activity after the test?
- Did you ever spend several days of *meaningful conversation* with your teacher and fellow students about the fact that the results of the test showed how it could be used for planning? For evaluation? Were you reassured that these results are not a threat?
- Did you understand why you were taking this test or its value to you **and** your teacher?

I seriously doubt it.

Before leaving this chapter, we will firmly establish how to make all tests and measurements an important and even enjoyable part of the learning process. We will make it easily understandable to teachers, administrators, students, and parents alike. In many ways, tests and measurements will become a critical catalyst to both the **success of the teaching process** and of the **student's understanding of the curriculum content.** Even though the content of the lesson—the subject being presented—will always be the body, the test and measurement tools will become the reoccurring, timely, diagnostic backbone.

When properly constructed and properly used, tests serve several functions. They evaluate the level to which the student understood and absorbed the *content* and *intent* of the lesson, the success of the teaching process. Additionally, the results show the teacher's efficiency, and will identify individual items that need attention or deletion. Both the teacher and the student can be immediately evaluated and adjustments can be made at every interval of the learning process in real time rather than in six-or eight-month intervals. Before the class moves forward, we must verify that this lesson has built the foundation for the next lesson.

- If the overwhelming value of a test and its results were understood **by educators**, teachers would eagerly close every lesson with a well-thought-out, relatively short quiz.
- If the overwhelming value of a test and its results were understood **by students**, they too would look forward to the immediate feedback and diagnostic value of the quiz.
- In both cases, tests and measurements would be viewed as constructive, meaningful, even exciting exercises, available in real time.

Before standardized tests can do anything toward improving education, students' attitudes toward (and understanding of) the whole test and measurement concept must be drastically enhanced. Students' understanding of the reason for and use of tests will directly affect their attitude and therefore their performance on tests.

The adoption of the practices we are going to discuss can easily revitalize the American classroom; *revitalize it at practically no expense.*

II. Administrators—from the building-level curriculum supervisor to the principal to the members of the board of education— should be equally ashamed of their misuse of this indispensable and highly creative tool. They feel a compelling need to justify the actions they take and the decisions they make, so they rely on the raw, frequently misunderstood, and consistently misused scores.

This misuse is not difficult to understand.

1. It's quick!
2. It's available!
3. It's visual!
4. It's comfortable!
5. It's traditional! And basically,
6. It's easy!

- It is simple to use the increase or decline of some number (score) to rationalize, even justify, your decision. It is *so* easy that educators have developed an in-depth bureaucracy, falsely implying that these numbers measures how children learn—and recently, how teachers teach.
- It is much simpler to assume or imply that this change in the numbers means something than it is to become a professional authority on tests and measurements. Learning this would allow you to hire and fire based on new criteria and understanding, based on something by which decisions can accurately be made, and classroom practices modified and improved.
- Even college professors who teach test and measurement classes *do not use* proven measurement practices. Some of our most prestigious colleges mark on a curve while (at the very same time) others of equal prestige are strictly 70, 80, 90, 100 graders.
- ***It is easier to compare hard numbers (even if they are meaningless) than it is to study and comprehend the critical lessons learned from the proper development and use of well-designed test and measurement instruments.*** It is undeniable that the prep time is exponentially higher. It is equally undeniable that the results are astounding.

It is so much easier to justify your decisions about teacher's retention, salary, promotion, and even the building of new schools and the budgets that support them when you can simply point to a change in the numbers.

All of the skills we are going to discuss are fundamental, easy to understand, easy to teach, and require no new budget entry. The only cost is time.

While we should not fault teachers or parents for not understanding these ideas—at least not up to now—I offer them this opportunity to become informed specialists on the art and techniques of developing and using test and measurement instruments. Doing it correctly is so rewarding it will put a smile on a teacher's face; it can actually be fun. Perhaps when the teachers in the classroom and the parents at the dinner table actually see the benefits of properly designed, administered, and evaluated tests, the boards of education and the administrative staff will awaken to this revitalization with a smile. Such understanding will revolutionize the how and where their money should be focused and redirect how policies should be written.

Unfortunately, for millions of students at every grade level, test and measurement instruments designed by the average teacher, professor, or administration **are inappropriate and frequently meaningless measurement devices.** Most tests measure neither the depth of the students' true knowledge nor the teachers' ability to present the subject effectively. The education system grossly obfuscates the nature, purpose, and most of all the value and power of a properly designed test instrument.

Please keep in mind that correcting this problem requires no more than a series of well-planned teachers' meetings and workshops. Districtwide train-the-trainer sessions can easily lead to school-based teach-the-teacher sessions.

This lack of understanding on the construction and use of a test causes unbelievable destruction. Tests are truly being used as a lunatic wields a hammer. They are weapons that threaten teachers to boost their classroom performance regardless of who they teach; weapons that signify the artificial closure of a learning unit to meet some trumped-up curriculum deadline; weapons to conveniently yet inappropriate imply academic achievement; weapons that confuse and ignore lasting experience, ability, achievement, interest, behavior, knowledge and even attitude toward school and learning.

Teachers, administrators, college admission officers, and scholarship boards must begin to give more thought to the design, appropriateness, and administration of currently used test and measurement devices, especially the standardized tests. At present, the extremely arbitrary assignment of some numeric ranking is worshiped as if it were an accurate measurement of a student's ability, a student's potential, or even a student's depth of learning. In most cases, it does not.

If teachers are never taught how to construct a good measurement device (be it a quiz, a test, or an exam), *and* they do not know how to use the results of these devices, *and* they do not understand how to assign a meaningful, unemotional, and unbiased interpretation to the results, then how (and what is worse, *why*) has such a monumental system of worshiping test results grown up around such arbitrary and unreliable data? It will quickly become evident to every teacher how the understanding of tests and measurements will be to the advantage of the entire educational process. Counting and reporting an X beside a question is so much easier than having to understand why the student got the question wrong.

For example, the Carnegie Unit, designed in 1906 at the request of the Carnegie Foundation to assist staff in the assignment of scholarship money (based on time in class and nothing more), has morphed from a simple arithmetic *indicator* into an authoritative *identifier* of one's intelligence and potential success. This numeric ranking aid maliciously grew into the driving force behind college admission, school system evaluation, student's placement, and even graduation. Here again, it's visual and it's easy.

A system designed to assist a clerk with day-to-day duties, grew into a doctrine that has been applied with religious fervor for over a century.

To add insult to this almost lethal injury, the unintended consequences of these frequently meaningless numbers are compared to other meaningless numbers in the same school, district, state, or nation, with no regard to individual environmental, social, or cultural differences of the student, the classroom composition, or the quality of the teacher. Differences in the sense of:

- teacher ability, preparation, or experience
- tax base per student
- class size
- material availability
- physical condition of the building
- socioeconomic conditions, especially parent involvement
- student's past experiences, and (very important)
- the unique learning styles of the individual student.

Too little thought is given to the validity of the test instrument itself as to whether it actually measures what the grade on the report card is purported to indicate. Youngsters with good memories can get an "A" in chemistry or geometry and not know a thing a year later. A "C" student may understand and use the information he or she has been exposed to for the rest of his or her life, despite weakness memorizing all the rules and regulations on which they were tested. When something is really learned—not memorized, but internalized—it becomes a part of who one is and how one thinks, and it is integrated into one's daily experiences. When things are purely memorized with little depth of understanding, they are easily forgotten.

Some students learn best through reading, some by hearing, some by seeing, and some by experiencing. Some students need more time to read a paragraph but retain 95 percent, while a fast reader finished in time, but retained only 55 percent. Are you aware of where each of your students fit on this spectrum?

I once took an eighth-grade test that contained one hundred questions. Being a slow and methodical reader, I only had thirty-seven of them finished when the time was up. Of the thirty-seven, I missed two. Thirty-five out of thirty-seven is a knowledge rate of 95 percent. In most circles, that's a solid A. I actually knew 95 percent of the questions I was asked **and had a chance to answer**.

I'm sure it is obvious by now that I received a solid F.

When I was in the eleventh grade, my father tried to discuss college admission with my guidance counselor. He told my Dad that if he had any money put away for my college education, that he should buy me a filling station because I would never make it through college. He justified that statement by saying "his test scores are consistently below average."

Years later, with a bachelor's degree and two master's degrees under my belt, I applied to graduate school to start on my doctorate. Amazingly, the university made me take a "remedial reading class" because my reading was deemed to be "slow." I took a class and failed it. I was refunded my money, and given a humorous reprimand from the instructor.

Follow this logic with me. Remember, this is a yet another true scenario.

A sentence flew rapidly across the screen on the front wall·
of the crowded classroom.

"Could anyone read that?" the teacher asked. No one raised
a hand.

"Could anyone get anything at all out of the sentence?" she
asked further.

I reluctantly raised my hand and said, "I saw the word *circus*."
The teacher was elated. She complimented me, proceeded
to slow the projector down just a trifle, and reran the same
sentence.

Again, no one raised a hand, apparently because no one
saw a thing at that speed. After a few seconds...

I again reluctantly raised my hand and said, "This time, I
saw the word *elephant*."

She almost had a meltdown. You would think I was going to
be the star pupil in her useless class.

She announced to the class—with great enthusiasm—that I
had "gotten the essence of the sentence." She led the class
in a round of unenthusiastic applause.

I interrupted her and said: "I'm sorry...but I know nothing
important about this sentence."

With great drama, she was taken aback.

"I have four children," I said. "If I'm going to take them to
this circus, I want to know if they **do** have an elephant or
do not have an elephant. Reading this fast, one misses too
much of the critical detail."

She was crushed.

This irreconcilable back and forth went on for several weeks
until her final testing declared that I had not improved my
reading skills. Therefore, I was eligible for a full refund. No one
ever mentioned that the result indicated that I was reading at a

ninth-grade level, but with a comprehension rate of 92 percent. The stars in the class, my peers, were reading at some arbitrary "graduate speed" and had a 63 percent retention rate. I just smiled and took the refund check.

It is important to understand (purely as an academic point of study) that I went on to graduate first in a class of thirty professionals, with my EdD, within the three years allotted for the program. I still read very methodically, one word carefully after another, which takes me a great deal of time.

I know a man with a high school diploma from a vocational school who worked in a lab with several PhDs. With serious dyslexia, he could learn very little through reading about viscosity or whatever was the problem of the day. However, when he sat with his understanding wife and listened to her read, he quickly became an indispensable part of a highly technical team of scientists. Remember, his test scores were low, and his reading speed was significantly below average, yet he was admired and was competing successfully with several respected, PhDs.

In another scenario, I had a young woman come in to my Capitol Hill office to apply for a job as a front-desk receptionist. After a brief interview, she took a typing skills test that I had advertised as having a minimum requirement of only thirty-five words per minute. (Honestly, I didn't even care how fast an applicant typed; at the time, it was simply an expected interview procedure.) When her time was up, she returned her paper, smiled, and said she thought she had topped thirty-five words per minute. In truth, she had. There was, however, a problem. There was *no* format to the letter: no salutation, very few spaces, no punctuation, incorrect capitalization, and very little proper spelling.

Reverting to my old classroom behavior, I realized that this was my fault. I never mentioned "words per minute" as a criterion again. I had expected much more, *none of which I had spelled out as my expectation.* I should not have assumed anything to be "understood." Every person comes to every event with different background experiences. We as educators must first evaluate where this person is in relation to where we think he or she should be. (Refer to Chapter I, "The Importance of Experience.")

Establishing specific goals and expectations is critical. How can you pack for a vacation if you don't know where you are going? How can you measure success (accomplishment) if you don't first know and make clear what you expect?

Every student comes into your class and approaches each new lesson with different levels of background experiences. These experiences must be sought out and understood by you in advance, enabling you to set *your* expectations and to adjust your approach, your vocabulary, and, most crucially, the setup of the lesson you're about to approach.

Our institutions of higher education, which have the responsibility for training our teachers, must do a better job. One of the most important is the development and administration of improved test and measurement classes. Here, we will review the very basic covenants for the physical and contextual structure of a measurement tool. *We will come to a strong, calculated, in-depth understanding of the purpose behind the construction and administration of the test, and the valuable use of the test's results.*

Unfortunately, those principles are being disregarded, and *most educators don't even seem to be aware that there is a problem.* It is unconscionable that school systems have such a shallow understanding of the very tools that produce the scores upon which teachers and students are measured and the system is funded, and around which the education system (unfortunately) revolves.

Teaching to the Test

With some amusement, I recall the embarrassment I felt the very first time I heard a national news report that some school district was being reprimanded for "teaching to the test." Along with everyone else listening, I jumped to the conclusion that there was some mischief going on—something underhanded—something not to be tolerated—even perhaps punishable. How, I thought, could my beloved public school system do something so dishonorable?

After a few minutes of thought, and after recalling my experiences in the classroom, I recalled the logic I always used. The test must be developed *first.* The test identifies, in small, specific bites, exactly what it is that I want my students to know when the lesson is over. The content of that test becomes the required curriculum content. The logical sequence becomes apparent, and the lesson plan falls out effortlessly.

Not only must the test instrument be developed first, it should consume the majority of the thought and time in designing a learning module or lesson plan. When you have identified every question you think a student should be able to answer at the end of the module—let's say, "What were the main causes leading up to WWII?"—then every conversation, exercise, picture, field trip, experience, and guest speaker should be enabling the student to understand and internalize, "What were the main causes leading up to WWII?" At the end of the unit, perhaps you would ask:

- What other nations were involved in WWII and what was their relationship to the United States at the time?
- What was going on in those nations that allowed such a conflict to arise?
- What was the time span of the US involvement from start to finish?
- How many leading causes have been identified by scholars?

- Can you identify the top leaders in each of the nations involved?
- Approximately how many people were killed in each country?
- Was there any one event that caused US involvement in the war?
- Was there any one event that stopped the US involvement in the war?
- Was there any one event for which that war is remembered?
- Did anything good come out of the war effort?

I can go on and on with six or eight other relevant questions that I think the student should know at the conclusion of the module on WWII. I'm sure you understand the idea. With those questions now identified by you (or the district) as being important enough to know, you can now begin to start a lesson plan, thinking through "How am I going to present these identified reference points?"

I must select activities, videos, readings, or speakers I can use to present this information, information that I have predetermined to be sufficiently critical to be on the final exam.

Is this "teaching to the test"? **I certainly hope so!**

If a hospital internist is going to take out a child's appendix, it would be my strong desire that someone had taught the young doctor a lesson on how to surgically remove an appendix. Was that lesson in violation of some mysterious ethic…or was someone teaching the test?

I recall one question on a statewide standardized test that asked:

"Pants are to knickers as a jacket is to:

a. *a pair of gloves*
b. *a warm hat*
c. *a coat*
d. *pajamas."*

I contacted the dignitaries at a large, prestigious East Coast university that designs the test instrument about my concerns to this and many similar questions. When I objected to the relevance of the word "knickers" to ninth-grade city students, I was told: ***"If the student had read Dickens, he or she would know what knickers are."***

"Oh, crap!" I thought. "Now they've got me. I've never read Dickens." They seemed to take pride in the "Gotcha!'" effect.

If I were a teacher who knew that his question was going to be asked of my students, you'd better believe that we would have a story, a poem, or some reference to knickers prior to the test.

Is that teaching to the test? Is that cheating?

Remember, tests are supposed to review the material covered in some prior lesson. Never having had a lesson—or experience—containing the word knickers, should eliminate your obligation to be evaluated on such a question. It also violates the very premise of how and why tests are to be derived, designed, and used.

Note: It is critical that we understand that I am not referring to being given the answers to the questions or memorizing the answers on a local quiz or standardized test. That is worthless. Even when the purpose is to deduce an answer from a problem situation, we cannot expect untaught and inexperienced answers to be measurable. There is obviously nothing to be gained educationwise, never mind the unethical and immoral implications surrounding the practice of giving the answers vs. teaching to the test.

Let's suppose we are going to teach how to bake cookies to a seventh-grade family and consumer science class. You would never walk into the classroom without having thought through, "What am I going to expect them to get out of this module? What end result am I trying for?" This is the same as asking, "What questions am I going to put on their final exam?"

- What are the results/what are my expectations of this lesson? (It should be more than simply baking a batch of edible cookies.)
- They must understand the fundamental practice of the *preparation* necessary before cooking anything (or performing any life skill).
  1. Gathering the ingredients and utensils suggested in the recipe.
  2. Understanding what each ingredient and utensil does, including the proper pronunciation of each.
  3. Discussing possible substitutions or additions (With or without nuts? Baking soda vs. baking powder?).
  4. Itemizing what pans, mixers, measuring spoons, are needed, and then explaining how to use each one.
  5. Explaining the settings on the oven.
  6. Demonstrating how to read a recipe.

This fundamental thought process of planning and thinking about the desired result, with its need for sequential processing and attention to detail, is all transferable knowledge. These are steps toward cause-and-effect relationships and toward wisdom that only comes in repeated tiny lessons and diversified experiences.

- Now, having spent quality time on thinking through the classroom activities, anticipating what experiences this particular lesson needs to make it understandable, and trying to anticipate any unusual events or activities, you have developed the content of the quiz, test, or exam. By virtue of thinking, "What questions am I going to ask the students when they finish?" you are now free to develop the step-by-step process by which you move the students to that level of understanding—a level that meets your now *predefined expectations.* You have developed the basis for your test questions and defined the steps you must take to get there.

By having thought through to the conclusion *first,* you can easily lay out the process—the lesson plan.

Are you teaching to the test?
Is this a criticism or a compliment?

Army Style

How would this work?

"OK, soldiers. Today we're going to become familiar with your rifle. I haven't decided yet exactly what I'll be evaluating you on. I hope you can figure this one out, because I've never done this before.

"Oh! You'd better pass the test too, or we'll have to do it over again. What's worse, if you don't pass, I'll get a cut in pay. Now go ahead and let's get started."

Alternatively, say this:

"OK, soldiers. When you finish this lesson, you will have learned how to take apart, clean, possibly repair, and reassemble your rifle. Listen up. That's:

- Take apart,
- Clean,
- Possibly repair, and
- Reassemble.

"We will try to get most of it finished within a three-minute period because you will need this speed and accuracy as a survival skill if you're under fire.

"It is possible that your rifle may jam or misfire when it gets hot from rapid firing. It may get sand or grit in its moving parts. It will become critical to you and your buddies that you understand how to disassemble it, clean it, repair it, and get it back together quickly.

"Let's review for a minute or two why this lesson may be worth your time."

The sergeant then proceeds to guide the class through the lesson using skills he or she, as the instructor, has already mastered prior to the class and guiding them in a sequence critical to the success of the predefined expectations.

Here again, it's worth considering: Is the sergeant teaching to the test?

The Measurement Instrument

There are several different styles of measurement tools; some are more useful than others; but each has its place. Let's think through multiple choice, true or false, fill in the blank, essay, oral, or performance based.

A variety should be used frequently. Sometimes, only one or two questions at the end of the class can establish and reinforce the main points of the lesson just completed. It will help the teacher know if the lesson was a success or not, and help students to understand their readiness to move to the next lesson. As a system, too often we move to the next lesson without understating or even caring that we may be building on a weak foundation.

Scheduling the carpenters to start building on Thursday morning assumes that the masons have finished the foundation and the mortar has dried. If they haven't finished, and if the mortar is not dry, you simply cannot proceed. How dare we be so foolish as to violate that elementary logic with our students?

Multiple Choice

A multiple-choice test is only of value if the teacher has given careful thought to the selection of the options. There should be at least three or four choices. The alternatives to the correct item should be, in some way, relevant—i.e., somewhere near right, or at least a possibility. One conspicuously correct answer and several obviously incorrect answers is nothing more than a parlor game. It will yield no relevant insight into either their learning or your teaching of the subject.

> Q: At what temperature should today's cookies be baked?
> a. 2,500°　　b. 350°　　c. 4,000°　　d. 27°

Equally bad would be to have the temperatures extremely close. In some cases, a reasonable range may be meaningful unless the exact number is vital—as in a machined tolerance on a gauge vs. a blood pressure range.

True or False

Here, as it is in most cases, self-evident questions (as in the first example here) should be avoided.

> Q: WWII was a battle fought between Canada and the United States. T/F
> vs.
> Q: Canada refused to fight alongside the United States during WWII. T/F

Answers must be thought through carefully and be reasonable. They can be general or specific depending on the need for detail of the subject. This is not an exercise where you can skimp on time just to get something on paper and have an easy-to-grade instrument. You are trying to diagnose a student's mastery of the topic—not the odds of flipping a coin.

Drawing Conclusions

You will be searching for an accurate answer that indicates the student understands a process after drawing a logical conclusion from the information you give them. Even if this *specific* detail was never presented in class, students are given enough information on the test to figure the correct answer if they have mastered the thinking process.

Q: If Mary had six eggs in her basket and she broke two, but she found three more in the hen house, how many unbroken eggs did she have in her basket? Answer: _________

You don't care if she did this problem in her head or on a scrap of paper. You are looking for the number 7.

Notice that you are establishing several things:

1. The student's ability to *comprehend a situation* by *reading* the scenario.
2. The student's ability to *convert* a word problem into an arithmetic problem.
3. The student's ability to *calculate* elementary math problems.
4. The student's skill of *deduction.*

In Chapter IV on diagnostic and prescriptive learning, we will discuss that the value in this question may be far more than 7. The value may well be in the discussion that follows.

If a student missed the correct answer but reading the problem aloud enables the student to come up with the correct answer, he or she may have a reading problem and not an arithmetic problem.

If a student missed the correct answer but is able to do the arithmetic correctly when expressed in only a numeric format, he or she may have a problem with comprehension, understanding, deduction, *or* reading…but not arithmetic.

If a student missed the correct answer and cannot work through it under any scenario, then—as a good start—one of the students who did get the correct answer should be invited to tutor the pupil.

If several students missed the correct answer, tutoring may be offered by another student to the entire class, breaking down and explaining each logical step he or she went through to get the correct answer. Several of the students who got the problem right may tag-team the tutoring session. (These youngsters are now developing a comfort zone in social skills, speaking skills, teaching skills, self-confidence, cooperation, empathy, understanding, and all kinds of lifelong skills—none of which is in the math curriculum.)

If most of the class missed the correct answer, the teacher must evaluate the various learning problems, regroup the children by skills, and remediate the missing understanding. This one is a teacher problem. The teacher misjudged the class's preparedness for the lesson; misjudged the experiences the students brought to the lesson; was unable to define, explain, or present a logical lesson that could be understood by the majority of the class. The teacher has identified a weakness that he or she must address. This is no longer a student problem.

Here especially is where the teacher should not just assign a failing grade and move on. Rethink the situation, redesign the presentation, and deliver it in a different way. When most of the class misses the question, it's a presentation problem. When the teacher realizes this, redesigns a better way to present the lesson, and reevaluates the success of the revised presentation, the system now has a better teacher.

Fill in the Blank

The need for committing some identified pieces of information to memory is as equally critical as knowing how to figure out a problem or knowing where to find the answer. In this type, *specificity is required.*

I once had a sergeant assigned to teach geography to my freshman ROTC class. He had never been in a teaching position before. When he made up his first test, he fell into an all-too-familiar trap. He literally took a sentence from a footnote, printed in tiny font, copied it over as a question, leaving one word out, drew a blank for us to fill in with the "proper" (be it ever so irrelevant) word.

Q: There are ___ bushels of peanuts grown on each acre on the south side of mountains in Vietnam.

No one got the answer correct. Even though the question was taken from a footnote, it was never mentioned during class. Nothing was done about an entire class missing the same question. No teacher was reprimanded, no teaching skill was improved, no procedures for test development were changed, and no student grew in his understanding of the culture he was studying. The air force marked on a curve, so all was perceived to be well with the world. On the other hand, if that number of bushels had been critical to a service member's survival in Vietnam, the instructor had an obligation to either:

- Remind the class that information in the footnotes is critical, and it may be on the test for future chapters. Or…
- Review the importance of the footnoted material, plan to teach the point, and work its significance into the lesson plan.

Assuming either of these obligations from a sergeant on temporary duty, of course, is pure folly.

Essay

Sometimes, regardless of the subject, writing a paragraph (or even several paragraphs) is a strong and meaningful measurement device. The problem is that teachers often don't know how to score the assignment. Frequently I hear that "those kinds of tests take too long to check."

Should a higher grade be given for:

- Neatness?
- Penmanship?
- Length?
- Style?
- Spelling?

Yes to all. But...

Before you use essay-style questions on a test you must—during your planning phase—*clearly anticipate what you are looking for.* When you finish reading the student's response, you simply ask yourself, "Did the student show that he or she understands the essence of the lesson?" For example, if there were three main points presented in the lesson, were all three points addressed in the answer? If there was a specific sequence of events relevant to the situation, did the student understand and recall the sequence correctly? If there is a critical measurement, an important name, or anything specific (rather than conceptual), did the student identify that specific item and incorporate it correctly into the essay/paragraph?

If a student (by accident or design) only discussed one of the three points, regardless of how flowery, verbose, or neat the writing, he or she has only internalized one-third of the lesson. That is 33 percent and must not be considered a passing grade. This student did not master the three points you were trying to present.

<u>Do not use an essay-type question if you have not given it a great deal of forethought and are prepared to evaluate the response professionally.</u>

Oral or Performance Based

One good measurement with many residual benefits is to place twenty or thirty relevant questions on 3x5-inch cards and put them in a basket. Each student is allowed to blindly select a question, stand in front of the class, and deliver an answer. All sorts of games can be invented to assign points or rewards. Asking for help from the class loses points, giving help to the presenter transfers points, etc.

The student should be able to address the class in a clear, informed, articulate manner, defending his or her position on a controversial subject. Everything about the presentation should be discussed. The teacher and the class should both comment on posture, attitude, delivery, volume, diction, articulation, and logic flow. This same evaluation should be made regardless of the subject matter.

These cards can be drawn prior to the presentation or on the spot, with students responding extemporaneously to the question.

After each presentation, the class evaluates the answer *and* the presentation. Perhaps even consider assigning no grades. Perhaps everyone gets an apple.

- Imagine all of the skills you are offering.
- Imagine the fun the students are having.

- In what other class does one learn to offer constructive criticism?
- In what other class does one learn to accept constructive criticism?

Other examples might be the ability to play a difficult passage on the clarinet or use a lathe in shop to turn a baseball bat. In every case, teachers must first think what they want the results to be, and how they will know when expectations have been met.

Comprehensive education demands that every teacher pays attention to every skill an educated person should display. A teacher must not be conveniently limited to the narrow subject matter implied in the title of his or her class. A paragraph written in a history class must present information accurately, logically, and understandably—not just regurgitated names and dates. Correct formatting, spelling and punctuation must be every teacher's responsibility—not just relegated to English class.

⁓⦁⦁⦁⁓

As we presently know them, classrooms pay too much attention to the rewarding of short-term memory of bits and pieces of data and information while showing insufficient respect for the long-range use of and the interrelationships between those facts and concepts. How do these individual pieces relate to much larger and more complex situations? Tests, as presently used, *assign grades to disjointed pieces of information, which are memorized, restated, counted, recorded, and forgotten.* Without careful integration into life's needs, this never becomes wisdom. At best, it remains information; at worst, just data. A student with a firm grasp of a concept or a process will often be punished with a failing grade if he or she cannot remember the date of the event or the name of the person who invented the process.

At a recent class reunion, I was reminiscing with some classmates about our high school Latin class. While it appeared at the time that I was struggling with selected parts of the class, I had in fact learned and understood conjugation and tenses, prefixes and suffixes, word origins, and all manner of grammatical concepts never adequately taught by any of my English teachers. Additionally, I had developed a love for the mythology, history, and geography of the Roman Empire, never before presented as well by any other of my teachers. I had truly learned a variety of great lessons, which I cherish and use even today.

My friends, both of whom had received "A's", couldn't remember the Latin word for the chicken we were having at dinner, saw no relevance to the class they had taken, could not conjugate "amo, amas, amat" or "ero, eris, erit," or even remember what those conjugations translated into. They tried to make a joke out of my understanding and retaining what was clearly the teacher's intent, and for which sixty years earlier my short-term memorization was graded, and for which I, to this day, carry only a "C."

However, facts and short-term memory are:

- easier to parrot back by a student,
- simpler to develop a test around,
- easier to score,
- simpler and quicker to count and report, and (worst of all)
- faster to provide data from which to draw irrational comparisons and meaningless conclusions.

I was once asked to run a research project on dropouts for a large, affluent county school district. The administration hand-picked a committee for me to meet with, made up of football captains, drum majors, presidents of national honor societies, and others of similar behavior. They were somewhat annoyed at my unwillingness to accept their suggested committee as-is, but they yielded.

I selected and interviewed twenty dropouts who reportedly had IQ scores of 120 or better. (I am rarely impressed with IQ scores, but it was at the time the only variable available to select a sample group.) Without exception, I came to admire each of these youngsters. For my entire career, I have found that you can usually get a straight answer by simply asking the students. It was somewhat embarrassing to report their consensus.

1. The students were bored. (This was highest on the list of criticisms.) *"School is not interesting."*
2. They saw little connection between what they were doing in class, and skills they might need as adults. *"Classes were not relevant."*
3. Most thought they were as smart at their teachers. (*Note:* Here, I found that the teacher's inability to combat the challenges presented by these students was perceived to be proof that the teachers were dull. Teachers used their position to discipline such students rather than being challenged by any student venturing outside the box.) Here again, they unknowingly reinforced the need for the teacher to always be the subject-matter expert.
4. A few reported schedule conflicts between the need to work (sometimes the *desire* to work) and the required school attendance schedule.

Note: When I offered those students the possibility of a shortened school day with no extracurricular activities or electives, they lit up with excitement. When I proposed that to the school board, I was shot down unanimously. In some districts, this is finally changing. In several other countries, however, this has long been standard operating procedure.

Paraphrasing the unfortunate underlying feeling, these dropouts (all identified as being above average) thought that they were as smart at their teachers. This thinking would be impossible if:

1. all teachers become unquestionable experts in their field,
2. all teachers hone the art of teaching over lecturing, instructing, and disciplining, and the students participated in the item analysis and evaluation of the tests and exams, actually becoming an integral part of the learning process. (Discussed in Chapter III, "Item Analysis.")

Teaching is a complicated profession, but it must start with the teacher being a subject-matter expert. Math teachers should not major in education and take a few classes in math. They must be a math major with a few classes in education and a year's practice in an actual classroom, working with a seasoned mentor.

Unfortunately for us all, if a young adult graduated with honors in math, he or she would be snatched up and better compensated (sometimes quite generously) for working in business or industry. Somehow, we must overcome the irrational acceptance of quality teachers not being compensated for producing those very students who, in the first year of employment, will earn twice as much as their teacher. Throughout my entire career, I have watched excellent teachers driven into administration because it was the only path to a higher salary. Where is the intelligence behind that? (Discussed in Chapter V, "Parental Involvement.")

❦

Let us review the lessons of this chapter.

1. Test, quiz, and exam are not bad words. They should not conjure up fear, anxiety, or intimidation. They are critical tools of teaching and learning that must be mastered by every teacher as the backbone of every lesson plan and classroom procedure. They should be diagnostic and should yield constructive—not punitive—information.

2. You should understand what questions you expect your students to answer and the level of performance you expect them to accomplish before you start the lesson. You must establish and document this firmly and methodically *before the lesson plan is completed* or the class begins.

3. Be sure to formulate each objective in the curriculum into several well-thought-out questions. There is no *best format.* Multiple choice, true or false, fill-in-the-blank, essay and an oral/performance response should all be used frequently.

These are typical of the things you must think through before you prepare your lesson or begin your first class. At the conclusion of this thought process, you will have your lesson plan, your process/sequence, your exam formatted, and you will know that your teaching skills are about to become exceptionally improved.

Note: The tools discussed in this chapter are only a part of what you need in your tests and measurements toolbox. One of the most significant companion tools deals with the question of what to do with the raw numbers, the scores these instruments produce. You will start to feel that smile I frequently mentioned as you relate this chapter with the chapters on "Diagnostic and Prescriptive Learning" and "Item Analysis." Despite its demanding effort, high-quality, successful teaching can be fun and will result in lifelong rewards beyond your imagination.

CHAPTER III

UNDERSTANDING "ITEM ANALYSIS"

It would be professionally unethical and educationally unproductive for a teacher to prepare a ten-problem math quiz by randomly making up multiplication items using any indiscriminate numbers that came to mind. It is equally unprofessional to copy a sentence from a text, leave out a key word, and call it a fill-in-the-blank test item. Few things are less effective than thoughtless multiple-choice questions—if the word "question" is even used correctly here.

The design, structure, and content of *every test item* must have as its base a well-constructed, carefully calculated, and meaningful problem. Each item on a test must have as its purpose the ability to provide information about that specific problem. Each of these items must have been presented during the delivery of the lesson, delivered as a specific, meaningful piece of the grand scheme of the lesson. The development and designing of a test item is often an untaught skill by our teacher-training institutions, despite the criticality of it being a productive and invaluable measurement device.

First, *all* teachers (not just new teachers) must not only understand the technique of designing test items, but must also internalize the value and use of the results from this new, improved measurement tool.

Owning a hammer and chisel will not make you a sculptor. Being a sculptor without a hammer and a chisel is equally futile. Either way, nothing beautiful will result. That same artist, with proper tools and materials, used properly, is unstoppable.

Before we discuss the following sample multiplication quiz, please take the time to study the detail and structure of each of these ten multiplication problems. *Note:* Skipping the study of this exercise without a slow and methodical analysis of these sample items will not be to your advantage in understanding the reasoning behind the role of item analysis in test development. (Key immediately follows examples.)

<u>Sample Multiplication Quiz</u>

1) 2,134
 x 23

2) 2,045
 x 13

3) 5,261
 x 33

4) 3,005
 x 12

5) 4,978
 x 35

6) 5,401
 x 20

7) 4,623
 x 41

8) 2,050
 x 12

9) 7,910
 x 50

10) 7,092
 x 78

Can you find any similarities between or among the following groupings of problems?

A. Q 1, 3 & 7
B. Q 2, 4 & 8
C. Q 6 & 9
D. Q 9 & 10
E. Q 5 & 10

I hope you found the following relationships:

A. Problems 1, 3, and 7 are simple. They all deal with numbers of less than 7. By design, there are no 7s, 8s, 9s, or 0s in any of these three problems. With these items, we are measuring the student's ability to manage the technique of multiplying with a two-digit multiplier. By using lower numbers, we do not clutter the diagnosis by measuring the student's mastery of the higher multiplication tables. Our single purpose is to see if this student knows how to perform a basic task, a fundamental skill. In a class of twenty-five students, most of them should get these three items correct with little trouble.

B. Problems 2, 4, and 8 continue to use digits of less than 7 for similar reasons. In this set however, we introduce 0s. Notice that in the case of #4 we carefully included a pair of zeros, requiring a unique skill (which of course was carefully taught and discussed during the lesson).

C. Problems 6 and 9 now introduce zeros in *both* the multiplicand and the multiplier. This involves a significantly higher level of understanding. After the processing of the zero is mastered, one may be introduced to the shortcut of moving the multiplier over one space, thereby shortening the need for recording four zeros.

D. Problems 5 and 10 introduce the higher numbers (above 6). You will notice the digits 7, 8, and 9 in every problem. We are no longer testing the ability to do multiplication problems with two-digit multipliers; we are now starting to measure the mastery of the upper level of the multiplication tables.

E. Group 9 and 10 now require the mastery of higher digits *and* zeros. Be careful here. These two may require special attention and individual analysis and some careful redo planning for the follow-up lesson.

After the administration of this carefully designed measurement tool, our next important task it to use these data to provide information indicating (1) exactly where each student needs remedial help **and** (2) how well we taught the concepts we are measuring. This requires an item-by-item analysis. Assuming we have a class of twenty-five students, your analysis sheet might look something like the following sample. (This is only a suggestion. You should feel free to customize whatever format you find useful.)

The design and the process are somewhat time-consuming but critical. If you are diligent about carefully designing your measurement tools, you will be able to keep them brief, while still maintaining their value and integrity. Rethink how much depth we are able to diagnose via this ten-item multiplication quiz.

1. Design your analysis sheet, unique to the size of your class and the number of items on your quiz.
2. Check each paper. Look for and notate any unique idiosyncrasies for later personal reference.
3. Record the incorrect items *by student* and *by item*. Total the x's both horizontally and laterally.

You have now gathered the raw data for your analysis—your diagnosis. The beauty will be when you turn these data into useful information, and that information into knowledge.

Sample Item Analysis Sheet

Student ID	Item # 1	Item # 2	Item # 3	Item # 4	Item # 5	Item # 6	Item # 7	Item # 8	Item # 9	Item # 10	Total Incorrect by Student
1											0
2						x			x		2
3		x									1
4											0
5										x	1
6						x				x	2
7											0
8		x		x					x	x	4
9											0
10						x					1
11	x	x			x		x		x	x	6
12											0
13											0
14						x			x		2
15						x					1
16											0
17		x				x	x	x	x		5
18											0
19				x		x					2
20											0
21									x		1
22										x	1
23	x					x	x		x	x	5
24											0
25				x	x						2
Total Incorrect: by Item.	2	4	0	3	2	8	3	1	7	6	

Now that you have carefully recorded the details of each student and of each item:

- How does all this effort pay off?
- What is the process for turning these data into valuable information?

Always remember that the evaluation of these (or any numbers) is meaningless unless the individual items on the measurement instrument have been purposefully designed to measure something specific.

In the everyday hustle and bustle of classroom demands, it is easy to fall into the complacent trap that "I've got to throw a few numbers on a test for the end of the week review." The truth is that regardless of that hustle, you must take the time to design every item on a meaningful tool, or it ceases to become a tool for learning. Always remember that you are checking how well you delivered the message and how well it was received. Quick-and-dirty test preparation will not get you what you need.

For example, if your class is working on midlevel subtraction, and you throw some numbers on a page and call it a test, a problem might look like this:

Example 1. $ 2,731.14
                       -      270.04

It does have some imbedded zeros in it and does demand some borrowing skills. It is—at best—a fair item, but it could be much stronger. What value would that same problem have if you carefully changed four digits?

Example 2.

$$\begin{array}{r} \$\ \ 2{,}130.14 \\ -\ \ \ \ 270.35 \\ \hline \end{array}$$

Study what a difference these few calculated changes have made. They are so similar and yet so very different. By the additional thought required, you now have a much more sophisticated test item that still measures imbedded zeros, but also introduces a more complicated level of borrowing *from* zeros (assuming that you have thoroughly presented this unique skill).

No matter what type test item you are designing, it pays to give attention to detail. Always work through each answer yourself so as to anticipate where a conflict of any kind might arise. This way, you build the solution to that conflict into your lesson plan. Teach it carefully, or redesign the item more carefully.

It would probably be profitable for you to grab a piece of scrap paper and work through Examples 1 and 2 above. I hope that you will immediately see the nuances resulting from changing the four digits. Please always remember that if tests are to be truly used as tools of your trade, you must understand how to take care of them, keeping them honed and capable of doing their job.

The exact same logic applies even when you're not designing a math item. For instance, if you were working with a history class:

Example 3. What are some examples of the main causes of World War II? vs.

Example 4. Clearly identify three of the five main causes of World War II.

In Example 3, how would you grade the answer if the student wrote a rather lengthy response, but only included one of the five causes you presented in class? Did he or she meet your expectations? How would the student know what your expectations are?

In Example 4, not only does the student know exactly what you expect, he or she knows when your minimum expectations are met, ***and*** you have a template against which to rationalize the quality of the answer. Here too, you might offer extra points if the student recalls all five causes that you had presented in your lesson.

Simply throwing numbers or words on a piece of paper does not make a measurement tool. Rather, that would make—in every sense of the word—a weapon. The results of a sloppy quiz are harmless and useless *until they are reported.* The reader of that report will immediately jump to unjustified assumptions about the student's ability and the teacher's effectiveness. You need, and should be looking for, far more than the need to report useless grades.

The analysis process:

1. Study carefully the number of students who missed each item. Select the top three or four and see if they have anything in common. In our sample, we see that problems #6, #9, and #10 were missed disproportionately. When 35 percent of a class misses the same question, you have identified your first problem.

2. Start your analysis of the missed items by seeing if the grouping has anything in common. You will see that both #6 and #9 introduced the zero in both the multiplicand and the multiplier. Both #9 and #10 dealt with larger numbers, requiring a knowledge of the higher multiplication tables not required in earlier items.

3. Problem #2, you will notice, was missed by four students. In this problem, you first introduced the imbedded zero. Using student #17 (who missed #2) as an example, you should go to all of the other problems containing zeros to see if any other items containing imbedded zeros were missed by that same student. Observe that he or she also missed #6, #7, #8, and #9—four of which also had imbedded zeros.

For the sake of brevity, I will not go on and on with samples of individual analyses. I think the concept is by now fairly basic and understandable. Continuing using student #17, we have several options.

Traditionally, five incorrect out of ten items is 50 percent. No problem. Give him an "F" and move on. However, you are a professional educator and a teacher who understands and accepts your obligation to the student. You now know that student #17 is in serious need of two things:

1. Most conspicuously to understand multiplication when a zero is in either the multiplier or the multiplicand.
2. Memorization work with the multiplication tables using numbers above 6.

At this point:

- Here is where we separate the sheep from the goat.
- Here is where we separate the job from the profession.
- Here is where we separate the lecturer from the teacher.
- Here is where we separate the weapons from the tools.

Review what you may do with the information you now have available to you about student #17.

You can, as suggested, record an "F" and move on. "He should have learned his multiplication tables last year." Alternatively, you can realize that if *you* don't stop the problem right here and right now, it will never be fixed. You know that #17 is on a slippery slope to the bottom.

Here is a simple example of the difference between a weapon and a tool:

Is it my desire to administer a quiz that will identify #17 as a poor performer, an "F" student?

With one report, **you have the power** *to embarrass the kid, anger the parents, document the failure of all the instructional processes that went before, document your own failures, and at the same time firmly establish that #17 will never be able to master the identified skills of multiplication you know he or she needs to succeed.*

or

Somehow, by use of an aide, a parent, a peer, a student from an upper grade, a computer-assisted program, a carefully selected workbook, or by working through lunch, you will see that student #17 gets help and—in due time—be retested and reevaluated before moving on. With this new attitude and understanding, your only enemy will be time.

At this point, someone will explain to you how all these problems could be solved by allowing every fifth-grade student to use a calculator. There is a good possibility that the student already knows how to use an application on his or her smartphone to perform such multiplication tasks.

Here, as in so many areas of educating people of all ages, we must give thoughtful separation of *process* from *product.* If we are only interested in the correct answer—as from a graduate student in a lab working on a research project—the *product* is all we need and we don't care how the student gets it.

In the case of teaching multiplication skills to an elementary school classroom, *process* is infinitely more important than *product.* There is an indisputable amount of brain training, thinking, logic, rule application, memorization, and self-discipline learned in math—without which our graduate student would never have gotten to the research lab.

An apprentice carpenter must first learn to identify, sharpen, care for, and use a hand saw, even knowing that in due time he will be using a power saw on the construction site. Understanding the fundamentals to any skill is never a waste of time.

⸙

- Item analysis is a time-consuming task. It is only after you internalize its criticality that you will begin to see it as enjoyable and rewarding.
- Item analysis is the only way that you can know how well you are doing as the teacher and how well they are doing as your students.
- Item analysis it the only way that you can change the attitudes of both your students and their parents toward tests, quizzes, exams, and grades.
- Item analysis forces you to deliberately select every word and every numeral you use on a test. It is probably the first time you will be forced to realize the <u>purpose of each question</u> and the <u>power of the answer.</u>

Because the process is so time-consuming, your skill in packing meaning into every question becomes important. Volume has little value; in fact, volume may be detrimental. The quality of your design becomes integral to your success! Do not wait until you have a hundred things on your mind on which you'd like to check progress. That is fatal for you and the students. Take a reading of your progress frequently, just as you glance at the gas gauge frequently on a long trip. You have learned to do this because you know the consequence of not doing it.

If a student can articulate a theme in three or four paragraphs, intelligently pointing out two or three causes of the American Civil War, why do we measure the response by word count or number of pages? Are there any among us who do not remember the assignment to "fill the Blue Book" or "in 1,500 words or more…"?

Even totally written assignments, be they in paragraphs or only in sentences, must be subjected to the same design criteria and the same item analysis as we have been discussing. If you have tried to present certain points about the settlement of the American West, you should know and codify what the key points are. During your lesson preparation, you will surely have identified those points you want to make. At the completion of the unit called *Westward Ho,* your written exam (your measurement tool) must be explained so carefully that the student understands your expectations. Each of those points you thought you were teaching had a theme, a content—all of which can be measured. Your question could be worded: "1) Please list the five reasons we discussed for why so many people decided to leave home to settle the American West." Additionally, "2) Please explain in detail at least three of the five reasons those settlers headed west." "3) Write one paragraph describing the hardships these travelers experienced on their trip and the significance of each."

Your item analysis of this type of exam is conceptually the same as it would be for a math test. You must identify what they know and what they have missed ***as related to your original intentions and identified expectations.*** Likewise, you then identify the areas and groups of weakness and work toward remediating the missed information.

Remedial Assistance

These two words—remedial assistance—are fraught with hidden problems and are most often the flaw in the fabric of item analysis. In Chapter IV, "Diagnostic and Prescriptive Learning," you will see the need for such detailed analysis. The most tedious problem with implementing this level of good practice is the personal time it requires. Teachers must be given the time to do what they should be expected to do, without hours and hours of homework.

Student #11 in our sample item analysis sheet is conspicuously the student in the class needing the most help. His basic skills with two-digit multipliers are very weak. You think you know how to help him but you only see him—along with twenty-four others—for one period a day. What happens to the other twenty-four students while you do one-on-one remediation with student #11? Yet, with this student, it's pay now or pay later.

For one decade of my career as an educator, I was the band director of a highly respected high school concert band. Due to the difficulty of the music being performed, oftentimes individuals and even entire instrument sections had serious mastery problems with selected passages, notes, or techniques. In those cases, the item analysis was (most of the time) conspicuous. It was not difficult to identify exactly who needed remedial assistance and exactly where. The resolution of the problem was clearly *one-on-one time with me.*

Before anything could be accomplished, there had to be an understanding that the only way for us to achieve perfection was to identify and remediate every tiny problem. It had to be understood that that is the way we grew as an organization. No one could be embarrassed, annoyed, or uncooperative. When a problem was identified and corrected, the entire band advanced, and they all understood that.

"How can I possibly find that much time?"

1) Frequently, the student and I decided to eat in a hurry and sneak in a twenty-minute session during our thirty-minute lunch break. I found this to be very effective. ***Hint:*** In large schools in which there are several lunch periods scheduled each day, you might upstage the other teachers by arranging *your* planning period to coincide with all of

the lunch periods, freeing you from class obligations and allowing for one-on-ones every day.

2) On days when there was no regularly scheduled after-school halftime show practice or concert band rehearsal, I would have individuals (and sometimes entire sections) stay for an hour. That had to be carefully orchestrated with the parents dealing with rides and other family and work obligations. With individuals, I frequently provided the ride home. (That freedom has been somewhat restricted and caution is urged. Written permission may even be suggested if there is no overriding school policy.)

3) Some days, I would have the identified problem section all meet on the stage during their regularly scheduled band period. I would work with and focus only on the problem passages while a student conductor or drum major rehearsed the remaining members in less difficult selections. The two hidden benefits of such an arrangement were that the remaining members could easily see the value of the missing section and understand how critical the integration of each member and each section is to the success of the whole. Additionally, a student assisting me was given a real-life experience to develop and exercise skills and behaviors that might otherwise never be noticed, honed, or appreciated.

4) In many cases, first chair members were very competent and proficient on their instrument. (Just as you will have several students who stand out conspicuously ahead of the others in certain subject areas.) A part of the first chair's responsibility was to help see that everyone in the section would achieve a level of competence so as not to embarrass the rest. Often the five or six students in a section would be called together by the first chair to work on specific problem areas. It was common for me to see a senior player working

one-on-one, in a corner, before or after a rehearsal, with a peer who was having trouble with a passage. In a more academic setting, similar conventions can be held. Not only can peer counseling (within the class) be effective, but also students from upper grades (especially those with a hint of interest in a teaching career) can be helpful. These experiences are frequently reported by the students as extremely (sometimes unexpectedly) beneficial.

5) Where aides and parent helpers are available, they need to be used wisely. They should be focused on specific tasks rather than used only for baby-sitting functions. Carefully choreographed, volunteer parents might be called upon only when you have a student who needs help in a specific interest area or competency field: reading, math, music, etc. This kind of assistance is much more valuable than a bake sale at the PTA.

Not many years ago, I came across a ninth-grade boy who was bored to the point of distraction with his last period elective. His guidance counselor assigned him to assist in the handicapped wing as it was called at the time, working with younger special needs students under the direction of their teacher. One of the teachers there recognized his size, interest, talent, and demeanor, and started assigning him a few serious tasks.

Because this young man had enjoyed his experience so much, the following year he arranged for two periods a day working in a similar capacity. The staff and the students came to admire him and appreciate his being there. With only a little resistance from the administration, he was able to continue this schedule for his remaining years.

That young man, once perceived to be a discipline problem, is now finishing college at one of the better East Coast schools, majoring as a special education teacher. My talks with him frequently turn to graduate school and system-changing ideas he'd like to try.

There must be thousands of stories like this one. ***Students who are shy, bored, or misunderstood will often blossom when they are provided an alternative environment, shown some respect, and given some authority.*** Requesting some of these kids to help you with specifically diagnosed problems would be good for everyone involved. Embedded zeros can indeed be tricky.

<u>Regardless of how you frame the conversation, there is no value in diagnosing a student's weaknesses—by any means—unless you have strong, workable plans to remediate them.</u> Consider the fact that when a large percentage of the class has a similar weakness, the system has let them down. They have been allowed to get this far without anyone stopping long enough to get them back on track. It is up to you to reintroduce these missing lessons in a new, fresh, and understandable fashion. It is up to you to:

- diagnose their weaknesses,
- introduce remedial lessons,
- check your success,
- reevaluate their progress, and
- verify that they have succeeded

before you pass them on to the next teacher.

The Setup

Your job: Teach Jane how to build a birdhouse.

You must first think, "I wonder how much Jane already knows about birdhouses and carpentry tools?"

- Does she know exactly what a birdhouse is and how it relates to the nesting process?

- Does she understand how providing a birdhouse might benefit her backyard as well as the birds?
- Does she understand what skills you are going to teach her and how she may use them?
- What tools will she need to use to build a birdhouse?
- Does she know the name of each tool, what use it has, and how to use it correctly?
- Does she know what material the house will be made of and anything about the care of the material?
- Does she understand the different kinds of paint available and the value of each?
- Does she know what kind of birds in her area use birdhouses and what size the house and the opening must be?
- Does she understand that different birds have different requirements as to where the house is placed, how high it is placed, or how it is hung?

I'm sure you can expand this list, but I'm also sure that you get the idea. These types of questions *must* proceed any lesson plan. When the student is missing even just one of the items on your list, you must set them up before proceeding. Perhaps with Jane, the only discussion necessary is about paint. Perhaps other students need most of the items to be explained and set up. Finding out this information is not a test; it is simply the diagnostic measurement of the situation at hand, so you know how to proceed. You have no idea how to move forward if you don't first know where you are.

Now, with your workshop set up with all the tools and materials you will need, with the student having been familiarized with the tools she is going to be using, and with the reasons for the exercise established, you may start to teach the specific, sequential steps for building a birdhouse. Concurrent to the process, you will be teaching a dozen peripheral things. They too must be itemized. Such things as "how to use a brace and bit," "tool safety," "how to square a board," etc., must be identified in advance and documented. By doing this, you now have the backbone of your lesson plan as well as the skeleton for your tests and exams. This example is a performance-based lesson. Some of your tests will be written, some verbal, and some performance. You make your commonsense decision as directly related to the tasks. You can write about the difference between oil- and latex-based paint, but you should demonstrate your ability to square a board.

When the product is finished, the goal is reached, and you have observed and measured the success with which each step was demonstrated, your final test should be exactly parallel to the goals and tasks you identified in setting up the lesson.

Above all, understand that if the hole for the bird to get in is too small, and the perch is too short, then the birdhouse may be useless, *but the problem may not be with the student.*

Chapter IV

Diagnostic and Prescriptive Learning

In this chapter on diagnostic and prescriptive learning, we will discuss how to properly use the raw scores discussed in Chapter II, "Tests and Measurements." We are going to discuss how to use those raw numbers to the benefit of both the student and the teacher. We will see how using tests and measurements correctly will change tests from being perceived as threatening weapons to actually becoming valuable and constructive tools. The proper use of test scores will enable the test instruments to become a vital key to the revitalization of the American classroom. *We will discuss how bad test scores can make you the best teacher on the faculty; how incorrect answers will help to develop better students.*

I have been in meetings with executive boards of billion-dollar organizations where reports are given in glossy detail, and where everyone pretends to be involved and smilingly accepts the report as if they understood its significance, and where no one ever asks, "So what?"

In this chapter we will not only address the "So what?," we will also address the vast potential available from using the information in the report (the test results) to affect change.

<u>Expectations</u>

I was once called to a special meeting with my principal and curriculum supervisor because they were concerned that their analysis of my concert band gradebook indicated that my grades "bore no resemblance to a normal curve" and, in general, were far too high.

As I recall, I had only eighty-three students in concert band that year and, by my supervisor's logic, I should have had at least two Fs and several Ds. I was accused of being flip when I asked, "Have you ever heard a concert band with two "F" tuba players and a "D" percussion section?" Whether it is a concert band, a basketball team, or a science lab experiment, everyone must perform at or above average—at the very least, no one should be performing below average.

During a public band performance in front of a thousand people, there is no place to hide. I, and every student, am keenly aware that we are being tested and evaluated. As the graduates from our public schools leave the auditorium and step onto life's stage, they too have no place to hide. As and Fs alike show the world what we have taught them. What did it yield to invest thirteen years of their life and—in many cases—$100,000?

What my administrators didn't understand was that when I accepted the job as the band director, *I accepted the responsibility to set the performance standards—the goals toward which each individual student and the group as a unit would strive—and then to identify the tasks and spend the time necessary to achieve my predefined, agreed-upon goals.* Fortunately for all concerned, I could not put any "D" and "F" players in my desk drawer, as other subjects might do with bad papers on parents' night. Paraphrasing public radio personality Garrison Keillor, "All band children are above average."

Apart from group performances like band and theater, there are times and ways to hide many classroom failures from the public.

For example, the art department would not display the pencil etchings of disinterested or untalented students at the county fair. When this happens, however, no one wins! A poorly performing student needs more attention, and that attention is valuable only if it is specific to that student's weaknesses. Weaknesses can be remediated only after careful diagnosis or evaluation of performance data.

I assumed it was my responsibility to bring each (and collectively "all") of my band students up to an acceptable level of performance. There was no way that any one player could be sitting in the midst of the group, boldly blaring out or banging away at an "F" performance level.

Please understand, it was *my* responsibility to ensure that no one did. "No one," in this case, must mean "not even one." It had evidently become my responsibility to also teach that logic to my supervisory team. I spent ten years in that school, during which time I am sure I learned as much about teaching as my students did about music. I also learned a great deal about the hazards, advantages, and role of the administration.

As we both grew—the band as an organization and I as its director—we gained a well-respected reputation. We came from a blue-collar community, a lower-to-middle-socioeconomic environment, and yet the school received national recognition for its newspaper, its literary magazine, its vocational shop program, and its instrumental department (among other things). The faculty expected no less.

The important questions are "Why?" and "How?"

After our band received a superior rating at a statewide concert band competition, one of the adjudicators sent for me after the performance. He was a visiting, high-ranking college dignitary.

"Are you Shipley?"

"Yes, sir."

"Well, that was unbelievable! I must congratulate you! I would never have expected that quality of sound, that precision, that musicianship, from that blue-collar community."

Being very young, politically inexperienced, and with absolutely no forethought of sarcasm intended, I smiled and said, "Then you would never have gotten it."

Even with all of his credentials as an educator and musician, I'm reasonably sure that he never understood the depth of my response. The next day I was called into the principal's office to be reprimanded for my disrespect to the visiting professor. Even after my explanation, my principal and curriculum supervisor didn't get it.

If parents, administrators, the classroom teacher, and the student have all decided that a given topic or skill is one that the student wants or needs, then it must be presented effectively. The problem is that (notwithstanding truancy, misbehavior, etc.) an "F" is an *easy way out* for all concerned. Trying to prevent it takes a great deal of talent, experience, wisdom, serious planning, and long hours of hard work.

Imagine that there are twenty roofing companies in your city. Now imagine that two of them are "F" quality companies, staffed by real losers. Four of them put "D" quality roofs on doghouses, and a few are average. You have a difficult time finding three or four artisans who can diagnose your problem, have the skills and tools to remediate your problem, and guarantee their work. Your expectations are that if one advertises as a roofer, then that title comes with certain skills. Should not a graduate of a public school also carry a certain level of expectation?

It cannot be tolerated for a teacher to stand before a class and fumble through a book, trying to decide where today's lesson should start, or to scribble down five random questions and call it a test. Students spot such incompetence and lose respect for the teacher in a minute. That lack of respect affects every aspect of the class's behavior. State and district curriculum guides lay out broad goals and some tasks, but the implementation requires the teacher to skillfully plan, gather materials, sequence and coordinate each activity, and invest immeasurable time and energy. ***If teaching is not fun, rewarding, and exhausting, you're probably not doing it right.***

You must not only make a comprehensive, long-range plan of attack to each lesson, you must also develop the tests and measurements necessary to monitor your progress. You must gather the materials and prepare yourself to deliver your lesson with knowledge and enthusiasm.

- Subject expertise alone, without a practiced delivery, is not enough.
- Enthusiasm alone, without expertise and preparation, is not enough.
- Academic credentials alone, without experience, are not enough.
- Degrees must become evidence of mastery, not of time put in.

First, and most crucial to being successful, a teacher must know the subject so well that every event in the classroom, every comment by a troublemaker, every nuance of a slow learner, and every challenging question by an astute student can be related back to the subject with flair. Second, the teacher must then deliver interesting, informed, enthusiastic, and occasionally humorous presentations, both rehearsed and extemporaneously. This is possible only when backed by knowledge, experience, materials, and modeling.

On the subject of modeling, allow me to branch for a very short but relevant story.

After teaching at a large high school for ten years, and after having developed a superior music department—including a fine concert band—I accepted a promotion to be vice principal of a prestigious school in the next town.

I was replaced by a first-year teacher just out of college. Unfortunately for everyone, it was a college with a mediocre music department and a below-average concert band, in which his activity was minimal. (This background is critical because it speaks directly to his weakness in experience and expertise.)

Several months into the new school year, I received a call from my previous principal.

"Tommy, I have a big favor to ask. Can you come up and talk to the new band director? Things are really bad up here!"

"No, sir, I can't do that. But I will be glad to talk to my kids." (Understand that in a four-year high school, 75 percent of the new concert band director's students had been *my* students only the year before. They had experience performing in an exceptional program, and that should have been enough to carry the program forward for several years.)

We agreed to a date, and I arrived a few days later during the band period. I asked the new director to get a cup of coffee in the faculty lounge, and I seated myself on the conductor's stool, up on the podium where I had previously sat for a decade. The silence was conspicuous. What were they expecting me to say?

I learned that the drum major (with no training in 3/4 time) had led the National Anthem at a public performance in 2/4 time; that the trombones once went onto the football field without their mouthpieces; and that no one ever took music home to practice. *The band room was in disarray and music was laying helter-skelter all over the room.* (I cringed at the loss of formality, discipline, and general loss of respect for the band program.)

I admitted to the students that I had never faced this kind of situation before, and that—frankly—I didn't know what to say. I asked the 75 percent from last year, "Why are you allowing yourselves to stoop this low? Aren't you embarrassed?"

Too quickly, it became obvious that sabotage was going on. They were trying to embarrass the new director so much that he would either quit or be fired. The shocking answers were (the order of response is important here):

"We don't like him!"

"He doesn't know what he's doing!"

They went on:

"When you were here, we did what we did for *you*. Do you think we like marching in a little league parade on Saturday morning and then rushing back to a halftime show at a football game in the afternoon?"

"You knew what you were doing."

"We knew we couldn't let you down."

Please understand, this story is not about my ego. I only mention it to make a point. I can report that the band director did not return for a second year, and that the music department has remained in significant decline for decades. *However,* on that day I received a terrific graduate course in classroom deportment for a teacher.

A teacher must set a standard, an expectation toward which every student feels a partnership. The goals must be clearly identified, achievable, and meaningful. The skill with which the teacher implements that plan is equally critical. ***The teacher must be—above all—an expert on his or her subject matter.*** Only then can you speak with authority and exude the excitement of the topic you are teaching. The students will soon feel and share in your enthusiasm and excitement. They will recognize and respect your authority. A somewhat ***unintentional benefit*** is that there are usually no discipline problems because the entire group is about the business of getting better at whatever it is you are trying to teach. Conversely, they will—without a doubt—spot your lack of preparation, and the results will be devastating. Believe it!

Special Note: In due time, when teaching skills have become second nature, teaching another subject—be it as a substitute teacher or filling in for an hour for a missing teacher—becomes easier. Those teaching skills and techniques are easily interchangeable. Only the expertise in the subject matter will take more time to prepare.

As vice principal, I was once asked to substitute for a teacher's sixth-period *Macbeth* class while she kept a dentist appointment. I prepared for the lesson on Shakespeare's tragic play as I would any other lesson, and truly enjoyed the experience. It took several hours at home for the one fifty-minute class.

Late the next afternoon, the teacher stormed into my office and said, "I'll never use you as a substitute again. The kids want you back as their teacher because they said, 'You make *Macbeth* fun.' Fun! Really!"

Currently, accepted logic from most educators is that beginning teachers must pay their dues. They tell them that the first year is the hardest. *I must suggest the contrary.*

My college experience was so comprehensive and so diversified that when I walked into my first-year classroom, it was simply an extension of what I had been doing in college. I never missed a beat. While I am not implying that I didn't improve greatly with each year's experience, neither my students nor my parents had any idea if I was a first-year teacher or an experienced trouper.

We must demand that teacher-training colleges be sure that this infamous first-year experience is absorbed into the student teacher experience; a for-credit, carefully monitored experience. ___**No group of youngsters should suffer from being an extension of a new teacher's learning experience.**___ It is unethical to do otherwise!

My announcement that I had decided to be a teacher was not received with the same enthusiasm shared by those who announce they are going to Harvard or MIT. Why this was so we will discuss in another chapter. That humiliation should never again be experienced by a budding teacher.

Note to first-year teachers: As each new year begins, last year's experiences, preparations, materials, and even jokes and anecdotes become easily available tools for this year's presentation. A comprehensive three-ring notebook kept and continually refined and updated is invaluable.

Everything we have discussed up to here is most productive when it is couched in the logic of diagnostic and prescriptive learning. The immediate problem is that most teachers don't understand the concept. In fact, many even unknowingly violate the logic that supports this concept every day.

I have actually seen band directors stand in front of a band and say (sometimes kindly and sometimes with anger), "That sounds terrible; now play it again."

- Exactly "what" sounds terrible?
- Exactly "how" should we "fix it"?
- Exactly how will we know when it is "fixed"?

I'm sure you have heard teachers of academic subjects make similar statements. "These papers are terrible! You all are simply not trying. What did you'all do in the fifth grade anyway?" Then, to add insult to this injury, they announce, "But we must move on."

Can you imagine a medical doctor standing in the waiting room of his office and shouting, "You people are all sick! Why didn't you take better care of yourselves? I'm really busy. I hope you all get well!"

Why, then, do we accept that behavior from our teachers? Mostly, because it takes a commitment to diagnostic and prescriptive thinking to implement the revitalization we are seeking. That commitment cannot be realized until each teacher understands the *purpose of* and the *power of* such a valuable teaching tool.

Please review for one moment. In each case, we must first set the standard, the goal, or the level of performance with which we will be satisfied. It may be the noncognitive skill of typing sixty words a minute, or the ability to play a sixteenth-note passage from a difficult symphonic overture. It may be the cognitive skill of trying to find the cause of a stomachache and restore a comfortable feeling, or it may be the ability to present evidence that convinces a jury of the innocence of a client.

In all cases, there must be a standard, a goal, a predetermined mark toward which we move. ***If there is no predetermined destination, you cannot establish a set of tasks that will get you there, nor will you be able to measure the degree of competence achieved. If you don't know exactly where you want to go, how will you know when you have arrived?***

A very basic draft of an outline might follow this logic:

I. Lesson Preparation
   A. Identify broad major goals and objectives. (Where do you want to go with this lesson? What points are you trying to make?)
   B. Identify what questions one would answer or what task one would have to perform to prove that your objectives were met. (How will you know when you get there?)
   C. Identify what steps, tasks, or activities one should experience in order to understand those predefined objectives. (What road must we take to get there?)
   D. Put these steps, tasks, and activities into a logical sequence/progression. (Plan your trip and anticipate probable stops and possible detours.)
   E. Gather the materials, sample stories, and models needed to support each task. This need not be a "thing"; it may be a well-prepared paragraph of explanation or even a short story. (How shall we travel? By what vehicle will we travel?)

II. Diagnose Readiness of Students

A. Review the lesson plan to select key words, skills, or concepts without which your lesson cannot succeed. Are the words and concepts you are about to use or skills you are about to demand within the comprehension, capability, and experiences of your class?

B. Design a brief paper-and-pencil, oral, or performance diagnostic measurement (a game, a test) that will evaluate the readiness of the individuals and identify any shortcomings.

C. Administer the diagnostic test and perform an item analysis—an individual appraisal that will identify groups of weaknesses.

D. Group class into areas of needs.

E. Remediate or introduce the missing items you have identified.

III. Lesson Presentation

A. Discuss with your students the identified goals and objectives. What is it you expect the students to know (or do) by the time the lesson is completed?

B. Discuss why the introduction of this lesson is significant. How will your students eventually use this information in an upcoming class—or in life skills?

C. Discuss the process by which you hope to lead the students to this conclusion (include your plans for activities, tests, and measurements).

D. Discuss what the class already knows about the broad objectives and make careful notes and observations about strengths or weaknesses of the class and of individuals.

E. Work through your sequential plan using all appropriate props and aids. Frequent discussions and exchanges are necessary here. Maintain a pleasant attitude, supported by energy, enthusiasm, and (above all) knowledge. Never try to fake your way through a lesson that you have never given before or rehearsed thoroughly. You will be spotted and disrespected.

F. Be ready, willing, and able to deviate from the plan as the class or individuals need.

IV. Lesson Evaluation

A. Review the original goals and tasks. Decide which ones are important enough to <u>commit to memory</u>, vs. <u>be familiar with</u>, or <u>know where to find.</u>

B. Using your predetermined questions or identified tasks (from I-B in this outline), develop a quiz, test, exam, or measurement appropriate to your expectations.

C. Administer the measurement after a brief explanation of what you expect and how you are going to use the results.

D. With the class (or, when appropriate, alone), perform an item analysis of the responses.

E. Identify those areas of mastery and those areas of weakness and/or lack of comprehension by individuals and/or by small groupings.

V. Lesson Conclusion

A. Using the information from the item analysis, determine what material needs to be retaught to which children.

B. Using peer help, groupings, teacher aides, individualized instruction, or parent assistants, rework the weak areas using new and different ideas, new examples, and new approaches. Do not repeat the same thing that didn't work the first time and expect a different result.

C. It is dangerous and self-defeating to move on too quickly to new material just to keep up with a curriculum guide. <u>It's simply pay now or pay later.</u>

D. You now have the data you need to evaluate *your* success as the one who delivered the lesson. Are there common themes evident? That is, did almost all of the class miss question #12? Where such indicators are evident, consider that your lesson presentation needs to be restructured, reworded, somehow "changed," and retaught.

Note: Explanations on how to develop a good measurement tool and how to use the results can be found in the chapters on "Tests and Measurements" and "Item Analysis."

The first step in diagnostic and prescriptive teaching is, therefore, the setting of the goal—the objective—the task to be accomplished. This standard should be stated in terms understandable to the class, the individuals, the parents, and the teacher. In both cognitive and noncognitive areas, the goal must be identified and clearly stated. It may be as easy as "to square and cut the end of a 1x6-inch board," or as complicated as "to investigate and report on the causes of the Second World War." The preparation for the lesson is the same.

The next step in the process is seeing how near to the goal the students already are before the lesson begins. It may be that they already know how to square and cut a board and no teaching is necessary. It may be that they have never seen a square. You must firmly establish if they are ready for the lesson.

Here is where we begin to separate the good teachers from the bad.

If the whole class is expected to move in lockstep through a curriculum guide, those who *already know* will get the same dose as those who *do not know*. Here, too, is where we begin to implement individualized instruction. If we don't, we deny the existence of individual differences in the experiences of our students. For lack of a better term, the device used to establish the readiness of the individuals, and of the class, might be called a "pretest." Recall: It probably shouldn't even be called a test, nor should the grades be recorded. The only reason a medical doctor would record your temperature on the first visit is to compare you to a pre-established standard or to use it to establish a baseline. There is no way that the results should be used as a punishment or a threat. It is simply the reading of one tool in the diagnostic process.

The development of the pretest is easy. After the goals have been established for the unit, the pretest will surface effortlessly from the specific steps already identified when setting up the goals. (Remember, the student will not understand a conversation about squaring off the end of a board if he or she has never seen or used a square. You must establish that level of experience before you proceed.)

If an English teacher is about to begin a six-week unit on punctuation, a good pretest will identify not only where the class is, but an item analysis will show exactly what skills each student is missing.

When, out of thirty students, the pretest showed that only two were having trouble with the use of the question mark, then only two should have to sit through the instructional unit on question marks. If one student has a perfect score, he or she may be asked to assist the two in need of the question mark unit. If this practice were against school or district policy, then assistance from an aide or a specially scheduled session with the teacher would prevent the other twenty-eight students from wasting time. (If peer assistance *is* against district policy, work toward changing the policy. Here, interpersonal relationships and social interplay are just as important to develop as facts, figures, and processes.)

The only time I ate in the school cafeteria was on the days when I had lunchroom duty. Most lunch periods were spent at my desk in a one-on-one with a student whom I had identified as having a unique problem—a problem that, if worked out during class time, would have required all of the rest of the class to sit and wait. They would have become disinterested, restless, and eventually discipline problems. With rare exceptions, this should be avoided. The momentum, the continuity, and the energy within the classroom are second only to the teacher's knowledge of the subject being presented. Deviations from a plan should be very brief, to the point, and never presented with a resentful attitude. Attitude and discipline problems can originate from boredom and from meaningless tasks inflicted on the whole class.

Naturally, it is easiest on the teacher if all thirty students in the class sit politely and give parrot-like responses to questions. It becomes work when thirty kids are at ten different stages at the same time.

- Adequate preparation is indispensable.
- Thorough follow through is time-consuming.
- The time and energy demands are exhausting!
- The rewards are unbelievable!

As previously mentioned, I did a study of dropouts who had IQs of 120 or better. (While I strongly oppose the use of IQs as single variables, I had no better measurement at that time.) The results showed that better than 80 percent of these youngsters thought they were "wasting their time," that they were "smarter than the teacher," and that they had "more interesting things to do." Unfortunately, as I talked with those bright youngsters I realized that the school system did not see them as voters, leaders, and taxpayers of the future. Today, the message from similar groups has not changed.

So far, we have had to think through what it is we want to accomplish. We have had to identify the steps to get to this end by making clear, specific progress statements identifying stepping-stones toward our goal. We have had to develop a brief pretest, administer it, analyze it (not "check it"), and organize our class into groups by need, and we have not *yet begun to teach.*

Our English teacher now sees that almost the whole class is weak on the use of the colon and the semicolon. She or he reviews the materials for excellent examples that will be in the students' classroom environment, their home, and their literature. With enthusiasm, they work through the lessons and, using visual and oral examples, develop an understanding of the usage of these two punctuation marks.

Since this specific skill must be committed to memory, since it cannot be looked up in a textbook for the rest of the student's life, it requires more than a where-to-find-it level of understanding. We must separate this must-be-memorized skill from a where-to-find-it skill, such as the atomic weight of gold—the memorization of which is far too often used as an indicator of one's ability to learn and understand chemistry.

In this latter situation, professionals (even serious students) who use the atomic weight of gold frequently need not memorize it. They must simply know where to find it. Those who use it repeatedly will, after several references to the atomic valence chart hanging on the lab wall in front of them, commit it unconsciously to memory. When any church organist plays "Amazing Grace" enough times, she or he will memorize it without effort. Forcing the unnecessary memorization of some things is an artificial and most often meaningless indication of one's ability. Here again, in most classrooms memorization is an easy thing to measure and report.

At the completion of a unit (a set of related goals), the teacher must measure not only what the students have learned, but also measure his or her own effectiveness. The results of well-designed diagnostic tools will isolate the unlearned tasks. These tasks should be regrouped into a follow-up unit, given fresh examples, and reintroduced before closing out the original unit. ***If the tasks were deliberately identified as needed skills, how can we continually move on knowing that the tasks have been missed?***

As professional educators, we must—at each grade level—hold ourselves responsible for having the subject knowledge, the teaching skills, and the professional attitude to see that each student comes up to a predetermined level of proficiency. Can you imagine a band director putting 125 students on the concert stage without the individual time and attention needed to see that each student rose to a predetermined level of proficiency? Why then should the math teacher do differently?

In the chapter on "Tests and Measurements," you will find simple guidelines for the design and use of these previously misused and misunderstood classroom tools. Special attention should be paid to Chapter III, "Item Analysis." Without some interest and involvement, it will be difficult for the average parent to evaluate the presence of and proper use of diagnostic and prescriptive teaching. On the other hand, a few very simple methods can be shared to show its worth. ***Understanding garners support.***

It is vital for both the child *and* the parent to be so familiar with diagnostic and prescriptive teaching that they can discuss it around the dinner table with some real and meaningful conversation about school. It would be healthy if the question from the parent, "How'd things go at school today?" could be answered in a complete sentence delivering meaningful information. The answer cannot continue to be, "Nothing much." Imagine where the education system would be if the parents of every child understood what the child was supposed to be learning and what progress they are making.

At that same table, if Junior had said, "Dad, the car's sounding a little funny and it doesn't have any pickup from a dead stop," you can bet that Dad would demand that the conversation develop into something far more than one-word responses. Why does a similar problem statement by Junior saying, "Mom, I hate my geometry teacher and I'm not getting whatever he is trying to teach" gets far less serious attention. It is usually followed by some traditional parent-generated cliché like, "I hated my geometry teacher, too" or "You'd better learn to like him."

Diagnostic and prescriptive teaching makes the class more interesting, it makes lessons more understandable, and it makes tests less threatening. In a good working environment, the following signs should be observed and the following questions asked:

- Does the teacher explain, discuss, and provide a list of things being covered in the next lesson or unit?
- Are the students encouraged to share and discuss that list with their parents?
- Does the class discuss the answers to the related quiz or test after it's been returned?
- Is homework assigned where necessary, collected, graded, and discussed?
- Do the teacher, the students, and the parents understand what item analysis is and how it supports class activities?
- Are missed test items identified, retaught, and retested before moving to the next unit?

Without diagnostic and prescriptive teaching as a base, there will continue to be an arrogant misuse of authority disguised as "teaching." Properly designed exams are tools to measure the teacher as well as the student. (The same cannot be said for standardized tests!)

CHAPTER V

PARENTAL INVOLVEMENT AND FAMILY INFLUENCES

...breaking the cycle

Parental involvement in a child's education manifests itself in a wide variety of expressions. I have seen it range from total neglect to overbearing annoyance. Parents find a level of comfort suitable for them, usually based on the way they were raised. They do this even though they may have had no formal training on what is the most constructive style of involvement desirable. The style and degree of involvement will change as the student grows; the criticality of involvement remains undeniable.

It is not too early to start to support the child's academic development within the first months of his or her mother's pregnancy. The most obvious, and by some thinking the most important, is that parents (especially the mother) must stop smoking, drinking, and using drugs. Is this an educational issue? Evidence proves it is! The creation of a clean and healthy developmental environment for the budding student must not be underestimated. Evidence to the contrary is overwhelming. What exactly should one expect from chemical-contaminated blood, filthy air, and an unhealthy environment?

A healthy environment, love, and nurturing will give the baby a head start far beyond our previous understanding. Relaxing music accompanied by warm, gentle, hands-on massage of the growing belly, keeping time with the pulse of the music, talking and singing to the child: all should be done in the absence of stress and arguing. This, along with traditional twenty-first-century prenatal care, will yield amazing results that are obvious during the very first days spent with this newborn.

After childbirth, that nurturing should continue daily, from calm, warm, restful cuddling to talking, singing, reading, and playing with the baby. Always offering new experiences of things, colors, and shapes—making conversation about everything. Let the infant take the lead. Don't push. Children will let you know when they're tired. There should be lots of rest and free time to explore age-appropriate toys and stimulating surroundings. In due time, simple problem-solving experiences, toys, and situations—couched in an environment of love, stimulation, acceptance, nutrition, and careful roughhousing—can be slowly introduced with great patience.

While the practice of reading to a youngster is valid, I would prefer the practice to be changed to reading and discussing with the child. From this point forward, we must offer the child as many experiences as he or she is willing to absorb. Since every experience is new, each must be accompanied by an explanation: the what, where, why, or the name and use of the object being shown. Be careful to:

- Keep it short.
- Keep it fun.
- Make it rewarding.
- Never express anger, displeasure, or impatience.
- Show your acceptance and pleasure.

As learning is equated with pleasure and reward, it will become a self-fulfilling behavior. Do not take any of this to extremes! Be sure the child is happy, free, and enjoying life.

Therefore, the first level of parental Involvement deals with early one-on-one support. This may be the most important involvement parents will ever have. After school starts, the demands expand. *Expand*—not change—because all of the early behaviors must continue, somewhat reduced, but still be there. New opportunities for support will present themselves depending on the skills of the teacher and the personality of the student.

As mentioned previously, early in my career as an educator, it was my great pleasure to develop a high school instrumental music program. It was in a low-to-middle-socioeconomic community. The school's budget allowed only a pittance for operations: music, equipment, transportation, uniforms. Yet we had fine uniforms, all the music we needed, excellent percussion equipment, and all of the larger, costlier instruments not normally purchased by individuals, such as tubas, tympani, and bassoons.

Very shortly into my first year in that position, I realized the impossibility of building and maintaining a strong music program on a $250 annual budget. I called a meeting of the band members' parents, and explained to them that I would like to organize a group of parents for the sole purpose of band support. This Band Parents' Association was to have officers, hold business meetings and fundraising events, but above all, their children's band program needed financial support. I explained that we could not grow without an adequate library of both concert pieces *and* football music, without money for buses to parades and off-campus events, away games, and community activities. I explained that financial support for instrument repairs, drumheads, program printing, electronic tuners, music stands, and an array of similar things would contribute significantly toward a successful program.

I was able to explain—with as much tact as a twenty-two-year-old's experience would allow—that I did not need any help with being the band director, with teaching instrumental music to their kids, or with designing halftime shows. Rather, I said I only needed their support of the building effort they were about to experience. Not only their financial support, but also assistance with drivers, a first-aid team, chaperones, fundraisers, and trailer loaders. They not only agreed, they formed an efficient, textbook association rivaled by none at the time.

One of my strongest dads stepped forward at our first meeting and said, "We've never had a band director who knew how to pronounce *Debussy*. This man deserves our support!" (I only mention this here to reestablish what I firmly believe: You must always be the subject-matter expert; the authority; the role model.) You set the standard by which you plan to measure the students as individuals and the class as a dynamic whole. When you are recognized as the subject-matter expert, you will gain the respect of your students, your parents, and your peers. Discipline is minimized if not eliminated, and everything comes into focus.

The value of the Band Parents' Association became so obvious to the band members that when several of my students became band directors over the next decade at other schools, one of the conspicuous things I observed was their creation of a strong Band Parents' Association.

This is another example of how parent involvement can be extremely important to the success of your classroom activities, without you giving up any authority or responsibility in your role as the teacher in charge. Not one parent taught my drummers a new cadence for an upcoming parade or taught a difficult clarinet arpeggio to my first chair clarinetist. Parents, both as individuals and as a strong group, can provide immeasurable benefits to your classroom activities.

On the other hand, had there been a retired drummer from the nearby Naval Academy Band among my band parents, I would have welcomed and carefully used the assistance of such a talent. *You* must always maintain the authority over the role you are being paid to fill. *You* must gauge the ultimate wisdom behind every activity undertaken in your classroom, be it delivered by you, an aide, or a volunteer. With some luck, every classroom in your school will have a parent or two who has time to assist in an area with which you need help. Even though **they** have the time, **you** must develop and direct the talent. Perhaps they may offer some individual attention to a specific student or to a small group where a unique deficiency has been identified. That assistance is only productive when you have designed and explained the problem you are trying to solve *and* the remedial plan. In the absence of a paid position, there may be a local artist who would volunteer some time to help with sketching, shading, or watercolor landscapes. Planning a trip to a local museum and finding chaperones for that trip can be easily managed by most parents, allowing you the time to work with an individual or a small group requiring a higher level of training and experience.

One of the things to remember is that we must never confuse the skillful use of parental assistance with free professional help. These volunteers are not another teacher in the room. The identification of unique problems being experienced by a child and the individual remediation process must never be blindly handed over to anyone. The diagnosis of a student's level in any subject, the identification of where you want to take this child in that subject, the steps to get him or her there, and the continual evaluation of the student's progress are totally your responsibility. Your volunteers must have specific directions as to what you are trying to accomplish and how to get there, both of which have been carefully diagnosed and defined by you.

There are both horror stories and glorious praise for parental involvement. Is it actually overrated and unnecessary, or are there students who need individual attention and support that you simply can't get to because of time? Under the present short day of actual class time in most districts, and with the social demands competing for time and attention off campus, both homework and parental support present an interesting dichotomy.

Therefore, we see that—limited only by your imagination— the second kind of parental support is "the support of the broad classroom program."

⸺⊶⊷⸺

Another kind of support is what goes on *in the home*, outside the schoolhouse and the classroom, and possibly unrelated to your classroom activities. Regardless of the socioeconomic or cultural environment, there is, in many areas, a basic lack of home support. You can't expect to receive extra time for classroom volunteering from some unusually busy parents—especially single parents—when they barely have the time to earn a living, maintain a home, and raise a family. *The Revitalization of the American Classroom* is (understandably) not high on their to-do list. On the other hand, every home, every family, can be aware of the household's aura, the family's attitude toward the value of education. Understanding the role of education as a life-sustaining requirement, respect for teachers and the institution, and an interest in daily educational activities do not require a six-figure annual income or a college degree.

Note: The school, the classroom, and the teacher must be worthy of such respect. Unprepared teachers, foolish administrative policies and decisions, and poor physical environments are catalysts for discipline problems, attendance problems, and general disrespect. Unfortunately, I can take you to examples of all of these environments with little trouble.

While improving somewhat, there are still far too few families in which there is serious dinner table chatter centered around, "What did you do in school today?" (Here, some "parent education" may be needed to help them get around accepting "Nuthin" as an answer.)

I have observed that in far too many families, the parents—while giving lip service to the concept—have no idea where to start or how to help. Recall the chapter on the importance of experience. Many parents have had no experience or role models and do not know exactly what to do to support and assist their student. *An interested parent, exercising proper home support, is far more valuable than a parent at a PTA fundraiser or chaperoning a trip.* It would be time well spent if PTA meetings held workshops on "How to Support Your Student."

It is not as important—especially in the upper grades—for a parent to ask, "How may I help you with your homework?" Most parents couldn't help with calculus or trigonometry. It is critical that parents shows a sincere interest in and have a positive attitude toward education in general; that they show concern for the student's progress, and create an environment in which education is recognized, honored, and encouraged. Where such support exists, an environment is created in which what the teacher does in the classroom is respected and encouraged to be internalized and accepted as important.

Parents must make education a regular, normal, and important part of the day-to-day conversations and concerns of the family;

a priority for the assignment of time allocation and resources; and an understood and accepted part in the daily activities of the family unit. This aura of focused attention, care, and respect for education must start in preschool. Conversations about college or trade school or apprenticeships cannot start too soon. If a parent suddenly becomes concerned when his or her child is in the tenth grade, preaching and threats become meaningless. They will have some serious adjustments to make and remediation will be much more difficult...not to mention the time wasted prior to such a focused commitment.

- Is there daily reading going on (parents-to-youngster, youngster-to-parents, or personal)?
- Are there serious discussions about daily events (noisy TV cartoons vs. news)?
- Are cause-and-effect observations being pointed out and discussed in an interesting and nonthreatening manner?
  1. Possible repercussions of news events
  2. Geographic location of events
  3. Neighborhood situations
  4. Family problems
- Is there exposure to a wide variety of activities?
- How many times are there discussions about the consequences of decision making?

These are only a few examples of what a parent can do to stimulate the child's development and interest in learning. Parents do not have to show up at the school or attend a PTA meeting to be involved with their child's education. If baking a cake is a contribution parents would like to make, encourage them to have the child bake the cake *with* them—not watch TV in a separate room while the parent is busy in the kitchen. Parental Involvement takes many forms and must never be underestimated. Parents have had no lessons on what to do or how to focus their involvement. Are you prepared to guide them?

There are several criteria to consider when soliciting parental assistance. While awkward, these must be observed objectively and evaluated dispassionately. There is no room for emotion or soft social science when selecting whom you allow to work with your students—*even if these criteria may be perceived to be politically incorrect.* There are parents who lack certain characteristics that you must consider. Pay special attention to such things as:

- Behavior/attitude/personality
- Diction/pronunciation/articulation
- Vocabulary usage
- Rapport with students
- Hygiene (and finally, but not as critical are)
- Experience
- Education

I am referring to criteria associated with (and frequently attributed to) socioeconomic differences rather than ethnicity or race. Just because these differences are tolerated in your community does not mean that you should perpetuate them in the learning environment. Some characteristics need to be encouraged, and some eliminated. These are evident in the pool of volunteers from which you receive your students *and* from which you will seek classroom assistants. On the other hand, always find something for a volunteer to do, and show that he or she is appreciated. Working one-on-one with students (i.e., face time) does not have to be the only assignment for a willing volunteer.

(*Note:* For a variety of reasons, mitigation of these factors is far beyond the scope of this chapter. Just think through the disservice of exposing elementary students to poorly constructed sentences and mispronounced words from a well-intentioned volunteer.)

While there are certainly differences between cultural and ethnic groups that can be welcomed and accepted, there are some that should not. It is not your intent to make everyone "like me" or even "like each other." On the other hand, you should not yield to allowing the bar to be continually lowered. You should accept a broader responsibility not only for academic skills, but also for social graces, pronunciation, poise, articulation, and attitudes toward a culturally acceptable standard of behavior. Volunteers who cannot impart these characteristics will create a force that runs counter to your efforts.

It is your responsibility and must be your intention to bring every student up to a standard of education and social performance that will equip them for a successful career and meaningful relationships with friends, peers, and associates. Without serious understanding, acceptance, and purposeful intervention to the very cycle that created these unacceptable behaviors and allowed them to be passed on to the next generation, we will continue to stereotype ethnic and cultural behaviors as if they are a predetermined rather than a learned behavior. ***Repeatedly, we must address the need to break the various cycles into which society has allowed itself to regress.*** Misplaced volunteers (as well as poorly trained teachers) cannot—indeed, must not—be set up as role models.

Attitudes toward education are conspicuously higher in some family groups than they are in others. ***Your job is to be sure that you observe it, understand it, and prevent it from getting in the way on your never-ending efforts to break the cycle.*** Often, research looks only at single variables and proudly reports its misleading results. We must do everything we can to stop skin color, ethnicity, and neighborhood from being the variable that categorizes groups of students. Remember the phrase coined in Bill Clinton's presidential campaign in 1992: "It's the economy, stupid." Think about it! It drives education, too.

If you take a random group of fifty Asian American students from any large city school (with no regard for any criteria other than ethnicity), and you compare standardized test scores to a random group of fifty African American students from the same city, you can predict that the Asian group will test higher. The only variable mentioned here is ethnicity as the single variable separating the two groups.

- Can you therefore conclude that Asian Americans are smarter than African Americans?
- Is "blackness" the catalyst to lower test scores?
- Is there a cause-and-effect relationship?

Like it or not, that conclusion is what many average newspaper readers would take away from such a report, from such a comment in an article, regardless of its statistical accuracy. ***Far too many things are statistically valid when measured by a single variable, while at the same time being very unreliable.*** When something is unreliable, it may well be irrelevant. Bigots thrive on single-variable reporting!

Let us select a different group of fifty Asian American students. This time, all will be from single parent homes in which there are at least three siblings, none has a college education, and the household income in less than $20,000 a year. Now, let's select a new group of fifty African American students. Each comes from a two-parent household with a minimum of three siblings, where at least one parent has a doctorate, and the annual household income is $250,000 or more.

I invite you to reread those two short scenarios and tell me if you would now dare to make that same bet. Are you reluctant to bet on the rich black kids over the poor Asian kids? Didn't the first scenario imply that the Asians were "smarter"? ***There is strong evidence that families that are more socioeconomically successful tend to perpetuate the behaviors and attitudes that lead the next generation into similar levels of success.***

> Life imitating life...Behavior imitating behavior...
> Attitudes absorbing attitudes...
> Success based on Experience.

I (being a big city resident) recently stood behind a young mother in the checkout line at our local food market. She was in the late stages of pregnancy. Stretching up as high as he could reach was an eighteen-month-old trying in vain to hold his mother's hand, while a freewheeling three-year-old raised havoc with every candy bar in reach. The woman was simultaneously having an argument on her mobile phone with someone about a relationship problem that should not have been aired for public consumption.

The store clerk was having trouble with the balance available on the young mother's public assistance food card. She was asking her to select which items she did *not* want to purchase in order to lower her balance due. All the while, the mother was talking angrily on the phone in a volume more appropriate for a pep rally, while aiming her frustration and her tone of voice at the struggling cashier, who was trying valiantly to remain polite and patient. The three-year-old was blatantly stealing candy from the impulse-buying display shelf when her mother yelled, "You stupid Mother F..., don't you see dis place got cameras?" as she pointed to the ceiling. At that point, the younger of the children started to cry inconsolably, only to be yelled at with more profanity.

A heavyset man in line behind me shouted, "S'matter chew, Bitch?"...and I just melted into a puddle of discomfort. Are we all acting in a B-grade movie? Or is this my real world?

These are the children we must educate. This is the cycle we must break. Let us take a minute to consider why I shared this story with you:

1. What will you do if this mother offers to volunteer in your preschool class?
2. What will you do when this three-year-old girl yells an obscenity in your classroom?
3. How will you know what influencing experiences this child brings to your classroom?
4. Are your prepared to redirect her behaviors, attitudes, vocabulary, and education?
5. Even if you want to, is saving her within your scope? Your responsibility? Your ability?

Can this cycle be broken?

Note: During WWII, teachers were in great shortage. My mom's cousin was recruited early in the school year, and as a local homemaker—with only a high school education—came in to be our fourth-grade teacher. Before I learned this fact—when I was an adult teacher myself—I had always referred to her as one of the best teachers I ever had. She went on to retire from the county school system some thirty years later, with little college training and very little compensation. She loved the fourth graders, and the fourth graders loved her. If we were well behaved and caused no problems that day, she would turn down the lights, adjust the shades, move quietly to the front of the room, and read slowly from *Tom Sawyer* with all the drama and emotion of a Shakespearean actor. Those were the days before TV, so you can imagine with what wonder a good storyteller was held. With our heads down on our desks, we would hear

Miss Potee start: "Tom!...Tom!...What's gon' with that boy, I wonder? You Tom!"...and all was well. Each of us monitored the others to ensure that no kid or event would interrupt this very special time.

While understandable, there is very little discussion in most homes about what's actually going on in the classroom. If a parent shows interest every day, provides assistance and encouragement, monitors performance, facilitates scheduled obligations, praises, and knows when obligations are not being met, the young student soon absorbs a positive attitude, mimics the behavior, and understands the seriousness and expectations of the family toward education. ***Expectations must never be underestimated.*** (See Chapter IV, "Diagnostic and Prescriptive Teaching.")

In the elementary school years, if parents will reasonably and consistently limit and monitor social media and screen time; if they will help with basic things like spelling and arithmetic; and if they will work toward making education fun and rewarding, then they will establish productive daily habits and attitudes and set up expectations. With skillful mentoring and encouragement, education will become a valued and significant part of their daily life activities—a spontaneous part of their expectations and routine. Students must see their parents as knowledgeable role models and respected mentors. This is especially true in those areas requiring rote and memorization—like spelling and multiplication tables. (At the elementary school level, almost everyone can help with these fundamentals.) As students move into the upper grades, the actual academic assistance of their parents becomes less and less available—and, it is hoped, even less and less necessary. Not all parents can help directly with Algebra II or French IV. By that time, the love of and understanding of the need for learning should have been established. The parents' role evolves into one of daily "tapping the hoop"—the productive behavior will have become instinctive.

There have been revealing studies done on New York City cabdrivers who are bombarded relentlessly with stimulants to their brains. Results show that certain areas of their brains actually become larger and more active from the stimulation. Can you imagine having to hear, remember, and deliver your customers to different addresses every five or ten minutes? Can you imagine having to engage in wildly diverse chitchat and complaints with customers while contending with New York traffic, considering road closures and potential route changes, making those changes, and staying as civil as possible to the public? Imagine doing these things rapidly, hour after hour, day after day, for years.

Additional studies between violin players and other musicians reveal that the portion of the brain that controls the left hand of the violinist develops and is more active than the area that controls the right hand that holds the bow. (For non-musicians: every finger of the left hand must move in coordination with the other three. They must rapidly interpret and translate tiny notes into detailed, rapid, and specific movements and placement while undulating slightly on certain notes to provide the desired vibrato.)

In both studies, the same areas of the brain, stimulated by repetitive and aggressive activity, decrease in size and activity when the stimulation is removed. We must start explaining, rationalizing, and teaching the behavior we hope to develop very early. *We must be prepared to perpetuate that energy until the behavior we desire becomes automatic.*

When the home environment is one of modeling the young brain toward healthy attitudes and experiences dealing with education, the brain will respond in kind and reward the participant with involuntary growth and activity. *Reinforcement is self-fulfilling.* The brain's activities and capabilities will—absent any physical or medical interference—continue to grow in response to stimulants. (The frightening thing is that this works both ways!)

In situations where teachers have mastered their trade, have honed their skills, and have become true professionals, what goes on at home becomes less critical.* It is totally possible that the stimulation, the excitement for learning, the reward, may all come from the teacher in the classroom. There is little parental involvement with the drum major teaching the marching band the steps for the next halftime show, or the captain of the football team teaching a new diversionary move to his team. Yet, neither could be done by any student with more enthusiasm and with measurable success; neither activity could be teaching better life skills. Where did that motivation come from? Where did those skills come from?

One of my best and most successful musicians had no siblings, a father in jail for murder, and a mother who was a prostitute. How they got in that mess is far too long of a story for this chapter. My student went from being a potential dropout to a professional recording musician, all without any parental involvement or home support. In four years of high school, I never met either of his parents. In four years of high school, no one from his family ever attended a concert. Never underestimate your influence on your students' lives, even though you may not be aware of it until a conversation at the twenty-fifth high school reunion.

Home Environment

Recently I met two teenagers who have been allowed to become so socially unadjusted that I have serious doubts about their ability to ever fit in with fundamental societal norms. Pygmalion has never been needed as much as with these two young men. We are starting to see the results of generations being allowed to grow up with their eyes focused on a screen—first the TV and its vicious, violent video games, and now iPads and smartphone apps with versions of similar applications.

I am not implying that either of these boys is not keeping up with his school assignments. One is even an honor roll student. However, growing up and getting educated is about far more than learning the Three Rs. Personal interaction, socialization, conflict resolution, group dynamic, conversation, verbal interplay, and on and on are all conspicuously missing in these boys. I won't bore you with details of their behavior, but believe me when I use the words "totally socially unadjusted." With heads-down conversationless hours, and with little social interaction with peers, family, or relatives, these boys are destined to be misfits. Keep in mind that bad decisions made and people killed during "a game" *have no real consequence*. Switch off—switch on—and all is back to the status quo. One sixteen-year-old boy actually told me, "I'm not sure what my father does for a living, but I think he works somewhere in Annapolis."

How's that for dinner table conversation? How's that for parental involvement? How's that for role modeling? Moreover, whose fault is it?

At a recent social gathering, one tall, attractive teenager stood uncharacteristically sheepish behind his Dad. He seemed uninterested in interacting when engaged in fundamental social patter.

Uncle: "You're a senior this year. I hear you're doing well. Where are you going on to college?"

Teen, with head down, no eye contact, and lips hardly moving: "I'ownt' know." Translation: "I don't know."

Uncle: "Your Mom tells me you're good at video games. Maybe you could learn to design video games for some big company."

Teen: "Nah."
Translation: "I don't want to talk to you," and he walked away.

- It is easy for busy parents to be *uninvolved* when they have electronic babysitters, free of cost, already present in the house.
- It is easy for the school to accept (tolerate) this lack of parental involvement and the resulting behaviors. The criticality of adult social interplay and communication is grossly underestimated.
- It is so easy for us to pretend that "We'll get to it later," when in fact—in most cases—we won't, and it will affect the rest of the child's life. Have you ever heard a parent say, "He's too old for me to do anything with"?

Helping with Parental Involvement

Do your students' parents know when a new study unit is being introduced or whether there is anything they as a family can do to support it? How would they know what ideas to discuss around the dinner table or what experiences they may have had that can lead to reinforcement from home? Parents frequently know more about the child's cellphone plan limitations than they do about classroom expectations. Is this their fault? Or yours?

Do you send home a written prescription explaining what the upcoming unit is about, how it's important to the student, and what the parents can do to support the unit? You might stimulate involvement from the home by sending a very brief statement explaining the relevance of the upcoming lesson, the goal of the exercise, and several ways the family might support or encourage the unit.

Do you send home a prescription or an after-visit summary keeping parents appraised and involved with exciting plans, progress the class is making, or any course-correction ideas that may have come up?

> *Note:* Unfortunately, this takes even more work—***more time.*** Next to keeping up with your subject-matter education, honing your talent, and gaining valuable experience, ***time*** will be your biggest problem. To prepare a lesson properly, including all its interrelated parts, takes an inordinate amount of time.

I once taught a two-year class titled "Comparative Religion" to seventeen teenagers at a rural Methodist Church. It was a wonderful experience, and it included visits to other religions' worship services, guest speakers, in-depth conversations, and line-by-line comparisons of great books. One day after church, the minister said to me that he was receiving more comments about my Sunday school class than he was about his sermon. With no arrogance intended, I snapped back, "If you spent as much time on your sermon as I do on my lesson, maybe you would hear more."

It was common for me to spend five or six hours preparing a one-hour lesson, including a trip to the religion section of Baltimore's wonderful Pratt Public Library. Yet, at a local Saturday evening barbecue, the minister announced proudly, "It's getting late. I'd better get on to the office and prepare something for tomorrow's sermon."

If you are going to be a great teacher, time will be one of your biggest opponents.

Parental home involvement can start with simple, fundamental suggestions about the subject being presented in the upcoming lesson, to field trips, family stories or experiences, selected movies or TV shows, online research, etc. Always include a comment about the relevance of the lesson—the potential value in the life of the student. Do everything you can to gain the parent's understanding, respect, and support. Your efforts will be more effective if parents partner with you in the process, if they understand how to support your lesson plan. Knowing what you will be expecting of their child and where the lesson is heading, parents are better able and more interested in being a part of their child's education. That includes their gaining respect, admiration, and support for *you* as the subject-matter expert worthy of everyone's attention and cooperation.

Early in the school year, you might suggest that there be a globe or world map open and available near the TV, and that the evening news becomes a family event—if not nightly, at least several times a week. Whether it is a military coup or a tsunami, and whether it is directly related to school lessons or not, the location of each news item should be found on the map. If there was a tsunami, your planned lesson should be interrupted long enough for a meaningful classroom discussion about this event. Time set aside for current events is very productive! The long-range impact of such activities on students' attitudes toward learning and their awareness of the family's respect for learning are immeasurable. The knowledge range demanded for the informed citizenry you are preparing is far more than math, science, or a county championship.

If "foreign trade" was to be the topic for discussion in the class over the next few days, a good setup could be:

> "Tonight, when you get home, ask each member of your family to randomly select three items (a hot pad, a pair of shoes, a toy, a tool, etc.) from anywhere in the house. Then try to identify the country in which each is made. Keep a list and bring it with you to class tomorrow. We will group the items and make a graph. We will chart out where in the world the products we purchase are being made. We will locate each of those places on the world map and discuss how the results affect the US economy and US employment. If the data look interesting enough, we will ask the senior English class to prepare a presentation to the county newspaper."

As the home environment shows respect for and support of the pursuit of knowledge and the many interrelated values of education emerge, the student eventually becomes self-motivating. A parent doesn't have to be at the school and doesn't have to help Johnny with his homework every night to be supportive. Rather, by having two-way conversations, by providing meaningful examples, and by showing sincere interest, parents will have a significant and lasting influence on their student's school performance.

Always remember that the more educated the parents, the higher the level of assistance and involvement that occurs. We have strong evidence that families in which education is held on a conspicuously higher plane are more apt to produce the next generation of students who succeed. If youngsters have even hints of understanding that the position their parents are in—their living standards—results from their work ethic and possibly their education, then their attitude toward education starts out several steps above many of their fellow students.

On the other hand, never think for a moment that when that attention is missing, it dooms the student to failure. Attitudes and behaviors can be influenced and changed. Education seems to—at least, has a tendency to—perpetuate itself. *Whereas the opposite is also true.* Remember, poorly educated parents, parents who were unsuccessful with school, parents who goofed off all the way through high school, and parents who were never given the opportunity for an education, *do not have the same tendency* to push for and support education onto the next generation. Concurrently, the past education level of your students' parents does not prevent them from learning improved parenting skills or understanding what environment should be set up in the home to encourage educational success. The theme is not, "Someone must break this cycle." It is, "We must break this cycle."

We therefore have a dual scenario: parental involvement in the school and parental involvement in the home. Each has a specific value and each needs to be polished by you as the astute and concerned educator. The classroom is so much more dynamic than simply worrying about today's introductory lesson on punctuation or an upcoming standardized test.

⚬≈⚬

A Worrisome Aside

We have discussed the observation that socialization skills traditionally (previously) taught in the home are being sorely neglected—and in many cases are totally missing in some of the youngsters entering school. I mean missing "big time"—and worsening. These are skills and behaviors that, when neglected, can easily lead to rejection at a job interview or shunning at a social gathering of other educated people. (*Note:* Shunning frequently leads to seclusion and unhealthy attitude development.) ***Those who have poor social skills will only be accepted by others with equally poor social skills.*** Here, we witness the beginning of a new socioeconomic group with dubious expectations toward employment, lifestyle, and citizenship.

Will society expect schools to fill this gap too? Regardless of the magnitude of the current trend, there is a strong undercurrent of deterioration about which we must become concerned. ***Continuing to accept this lowering of the bar because we don't want to hurt anyone's feelings, we don't want to be politically incorrect, or don't want to embarrass anyone, will inevitably result in the entire social structure wallowing in the mud.*** These fears can preclude (indeed, prevent) much-needed honest conversation and academic debate. Well-meaning conversations quickly take on defensive emotion and a much-needed conclusion is never reached.

If a large percentage of the students consistently mispronounce a word, it is easier to allow the incorrect pronunciation to become acceptable—to lower the bar—than it is to take the time, talent, and effort to correct the entire population. Why? If most of the boys are inappropriately dressed, how can we justify not making that a school problem and correcting it? ***What service are we doing to the long-range development of the student's education by looking the other way?*** When the teaching of handwriting/penmanship became a lost art; when this generation of teachers can't even write script well themselves; when clerks and waiters have not been properly taught how to hold a pen—we have decided to correct that problem by eliminating handwriting and penmanship from the curriculum.

How many opportunities for parental involvement do we see in these few examples? Some may put away art supplies...another may bake a cake…help prep the ball field…or be aware of the child's total education and help reinforce the teacher's efforts.

Have you noticed such behaviors as:

- A lack of comfort in speaking/no conversational skills (both one-on-one and in groups)?
- Missing basic social manners, bad behavior?
- Poor posture/deportment/hygiene?
- Limited vocabulary/pronunciation/grammar?
- Inappropriate, unacceptable, uncomplimentary dress?

When, where, why, and how did we allow the pendulum to swing so far that correcting or even merely discussing these things in no longer an adult responsibility to the next generation? Parents and teachers must not allow themselves to be hamstrung by fear of crossing some arbitrary line of political correctness.

Since every family and every student is unique, generalizing about parental involvement as directly related to student success is a soft science. (*Note:* Fortunately, the research to establish this assumption as a fact is so basic that it would not take a very large grant to perform.) Nevertheless, repeated patterns do strongly suggest cause-and-effect relationships. Some of these have been observed thousands of times. It is not too difficult to make some assumptions from those numerous observations.

It is probably safe to assume, even with some caution, that:

- The *environment* and the *expectations* in the home of educated parents are more conducive to a child's success.
- Undereducated parents are not generally the best advocates for formal education. We must break this vicious cycle. We must sell education as the way out and the way up! If not academic skills, technical and vocational skills are fine!

- In any home, regardless of education or financial level, parents who show interest in and expose their children to such things as reading (from a very early age), travel, music, art, social skills, and serious conversations about current events and lifestyle topics are more apt to develop successful students. These students are vicariously having a world of experiences. As discussed in Chapter I, there is very little that is more important than experience.
- Parental involvement with a child *within the home* is significantly more important than the parents' attempts to help *within the school.*
- Parents can be shown (taught) these values through well-planned, formal training sessions. (Be careful: offering this training in broad, general terms at a PTA meeting may be much less effective.) ***The change in parental understanding and behavior brought about by the learning of new parenting skills will unquestionably improve the success of the student.***

Consider This Critical Point

A *great teacher* and an *interested student*—a student who buys into the program and who understands what he or she is embarking on—can team up and develop an Ivy League scholarship winner. They can do this even with the total absence of a storybook home environment or any parental involvement. I have seen it… I have done it… it's a fact.

A *dedicated parent* and a student can overcome a weak classroom environment and assure admittance into any college they set their minds to. They need not use the school as an excuse for the student's lack of accomplishment. This, too, I have witnessed.

However, I observe with equal conviction that a great teacher and a dedicated parent can do very little without a *committed student*. One way or another, someone (a teacher, parent, grandmother, minister, or neighbor) must invest the long-term and deliberate effort to help each youngster understand the need for a comprehensive education, and then guide the youngster along the path to get it. Without a *clear and deep-seated attitude* about education and all its ramifications—from preschool up—all will be lost. No amount of money, personal attention, time, or tears will produce a scholar. ***It may not be too long a stretch to think that attitude may move to the top of the list of criteria needed to grow an educated youngster—and a wise citizen.***

⸎

When parents offer more conversation, reading, travel, and experience of all kinds…
When there is understanding, involvement, reassurance, and support…
When there is a display of genuine interest in and for the value of education…
What a revitalization we will witness.

When the classroom experience becomes interesting, exciting, meaningful…
When the teacher earns respect by being the subject-matter authority, and is admired for being a kind, understanding, and respectful mentor…
What a revitalization we will see.

⸎

Personal note: Be sure you check with your senior administration before implementing any of these suggestions. Some districts and some unions make using parental assistance difficult. On the other hand, don't give in to your bureaucracy too easily. Parents can be your primary partners in the education process and should be constructively involved. You should be especially diligent in seeing that the research on the benefits of early (and continual) reading and family conversations about life and all its issues gets out to the parents of the younger children.

About the Author

Thomas Shipley comes to professional writing after several careers in which his technical and informative writing skills were critically honed. His credentials as an educator have been gathered from the University of Maryland, Loyola University, Nova University, and many graduate programs and advanced studies.

Thom's first career started as an educator in Anne Arundel County, Maryland, and ranged from being the first elementary instrumental music instructor on an eleven-school circuit to the high school band director and head of a respected music department at his alma mater, Glen Burnie High School. Thom was called to be vice principal of the prestigious Severna Park High School, from which he was promoted to become the first coordinator of educational information systems for the Anne Arundel County School System. After several years, his work was recognized by his being selected to be the first chief information officer for the Maryland State Department of Education. At the time of his retirement after thirty-one years of service, he was acting as an assistant superintendent of schools for the Maryland State Department of Education.

Three days after retiring from the State Department of Education, Thom was recruited to start his second career by accepting a position on Capitol Hill as the executive director of the National Association of Federally Impacted Schools, a new association of public schools dealing with federal funding for American Indian and military-dependent students. While there, he also became a consultant to the House and Senate Committees on Education. After growing that organization from thirty districts to over six hundred districts and from $400 million to $1.4 billion, he retired to become an entrepreneur.

Thom built custom homes and log cabins, owned and operated a beef, hog, and grain farm, purchased a national real estate franchise, and concurrently developed and operated a successful child development center and an assisted living facility for the elderly and mentally infirm. Thom also served on and chaired his county planning and zoning commission, directed ecumenical church choir cantatas, was guest conductor for high school and college musicals and concert performances, and became a certified family counselor. More recently, as a "rusty musician," he played and sang with the Baltimore Symphony Orchestra and was the guest conductor of the University of Maryland's impressive Symphonic Concert Band at their centennial celebration.

In 2000 Thom went to work for the Mid-Atlantic region of Kaiser Permanente. For the next twelve years, he was the liaison between the medical and administrative staffs at thirty-two medical facilities and the IT department. He retired from Kaiser Permanente in 2012 to try his hand at writing. He also mentors budding entrepreneurs at the University of Baltimore's School of Business.

Thom and his partner, Chris, have recently completed restoring and beautifully decorating a three-story stone-front Victorian row home in the cultural district of Baltimore's center city. He has published one small book, *Pop's Short Stories* (dedicated to his nine grandchildren and one great-granddaughter), and is working on another compilation that reflects his life experiences during the racial transitions of his youth.

© Thomas R. Shipley, EdD
thomshipleybooks@hotmail.com
www.thomshipleybooks.com

Made in the USA
Monee, IL
07 July 2026

56552686R00089